AMONG
THE ITALIAN
PARTISANS

AMONG THE ITALIAN PARTISANS

THE ALLIED CONTRIBUTION TO THE RESISTANCE

MALCOLM TUDOR

FONTHILL

*I would like to thank the former partisans, SOE and OSS agents,
airmen and other veterans of the war in Italy, together with their relatives,
who have provided me with information.*

Fonthill Media Language Policy

Fonthill Media publishes in the international English language market. One language edition
is published worldwide. As there are minor differences in spelling and presentation, especially
with regard to American English and British English, a policy is necessary to define which form
of English to use. The Fonthill Policy is to use the form of English native to the author. Malcolm
Tudor was born and educated in the United Kingdom and now lives in Newtown; therefore
British English has been adopted in this publication.

Fonthill Media Limited
Fonthill Media LLC
www.fonthillmedia.com
office@fonthillmedia.com

First published in the United Kingdom and the United States of America 2016

British Library Cataloguing in Publication Data:
A catalogue record for this book is available from the British Library

Typeset in 10pt on13pt Sabon
Printed and bound by CPI Group (UK) Ltd, Croydon, CR0 4YY

CONTENTS

Timeline

1939

3 September	Great Britain, France, Australia and New Zealand declare war on Germany. Italy remains neutral.

1940

10 June	Italy declares war on Great Britain and France.
3–19 August	Italian forces occupy British Somaliland.
13 September	Italians advance into Egypt.
9 December	The Successful British counter-offensive, Operation Compass, begins.

1941

January–May	Italy loses its East African Empire.
12 February	Rommel arrives in Libya as German forces join the war in North Africa.
11 December	Italy declares war on the United States.

1942

May–June	Axis (German and Italian) forces outflank the Gazala Line and take Tobruk.
23 October	Second Battle of El Alamein begins, leading to the eventual German and Italian retreat into Tunisia.
8 November	Allied invasion of Vichy French North Africa in Operation Torch.

1943

12–13 May	Surrender of all Axis forces in North Africa.
10 July–17 August	Allied landings and conquest of Sicily.
24–25 July	Mussolini deposed and replaced by Marshal Badoglio. The war continues alongside the German ally.
3 September	The 8th Army attacks across the Straits of Messina from Sicily in Operation Baytown. The Italians secretly sign terms of Armistice and Surrender with the Allies in Sicily.
8 September	The agreement is made public.
9 September	The main Allied landings at Salerno and Taranto. A Royalist government is soon set up at Brindisi. The Germans occupy the rest of the country.
12 September	Mussolini rescued from the Gran Sasso by German special forces. The puppet Italian Social Republic (RSI) is established at Salò.
1 October	Naples falls to the Allies with the help of a popular rising.
13 October	Italian Royalist government declares war on Germany and becomes a co-belligerent. The Gustav line is created by the Germans over the winter.

1944

4 June	The Allies take Rome.
11 July	An awards bureau for Italian helpers—the Allied Screening Commission—is created.
4 August	The 8th Army enters Florence.
September–December	The Allies advance beyond Massa in Tuscany and Rimini in the Romagna. The Germans establish a new defensive position, the Gothic Line, and the front is largely static over the winter.

1945

April	The Allied offensive resumes in the east and west.
2 May	German and Fascist forces surrender unconditionally after twenty months of war in Italy.

Glossary

A FORCE	The Allied deception and escape organisation.
AFHQ	Allied Force Headquarters, Mediterranean.
Alexander Certificate	The document awarded to Italians who assisted Allied personnel behind enemy lines following the armistice with Italy on 3 September 1943.
Allied Screening Commission	The awards bureau.
Geneva Convention	Relative to the treatment of prisoners of war, 1929; international humanitarian law.
Greater Germany	Germany and the states it annexed.
ICRC	International Committee of the Red Cross—the humanitarian agency and its HQ in Geneva, Switzerland. An intermediary and inspector in wartime.
ISLD	Inter-Services Liaison Department. The cover name for SIS.
IS9	The cover name for MI9 from 1944.
MI9	British Military Intelligence: escape and evasion.
MIS-X	United States Military Intelligence Section: escape and evasion. X was often used as a codeword for escape.
N SECTION	The escape and evasion section of A Force.

Nome di battaglia	The alias of a partisan or Allied agent. They are shown in brackets or inverted commas in this book.
No. 1 SPECIAL FORCE	Cover name for SOE in Italy.
OSS	United States Office of Strategic Services. The wartime intelligence agency and predecessor to the Central Intelligence Agency (CIA).
'Other Ranks'	Non-commissioned officers and privates in the forces of the United Kingdom and Commonwealth countries.
Prisoner of War (PoW)	A member of the armed forces captured by the enemy in the course of military operations. Also refers to captives who followed the armed forces without directly belonging to them—such as newspaper correspondents, providers of provisions, or contractors, provided they are in possession of an authorization from the military authorities.
Protecting Power	A neutral power that protects the interests of another in the territory of a third. In Italy this service was provided by the USA until 11 December 1941, and Switzerland thereafter.
SIS	British Secret Intelligence Service. Its Italian base at Bari was designated No. 1 Intelligence Unit.
Special Operations Executive (SOE)	British secret service—subversion and sabotage against the enemy overseas.
Successful escape or evasion	When the serviceman joined his own forces, or those of an allied power, or had left the territory of the detaining power, or of an ally of the power.
USAAF or AAF	The United States Army Air Forces; the military aviation service during the Second World War.
Wehrmacht	The unified armed forces of Germany, consisting of the *Heer* (Army), the *Kriegsmarine* (Navy), and the *Luftwaffe* (Air Force).

1
Unconventional Warfare

Italy provided fertile ground for unconventional warfare during the twenty months between Allied landings in the south on 3 September 1943 and the surrender of the German and Fascist armies on 2 May 1945. The covert actions were carried out by the partisans or by the forces of the Allied nations who were organised, trained and equipped for special operations.

The Italian Resistance movement went through all the classic stages of development—from passive acts to underground newspapers, escape lines, intelligence, sabotage, assassinations, guerrilla warfare, and, finally, a secret army.

The first partisan bands emerged in the mountains as a spontaneous reaction to the German takeover, and they were mainly composed of traditional anti-Fascists, disbanded Italian soldiers and escaped Allied prisoners of war. Groups and squads also carried out sabotage, recruitment and propaganda in the cities: *Gruppi di Azione Patriottica*, or 'GAP', and *Squadre di Azione Patriottica*, or 'SAP'. Networks such as the *Gruppi di Difesa della Donna* ('Women's Defence Groups') also encouraged rebellions against the authorities, provided assistance to the partisans, and organised public meetings to demand an end to the conflict. In addition, many women acted as couriers—known as '*staffette*'—or provided aid and comfort to disbanded Italian soldiers or escaped Allied prisoners of war.

In the autumn and winter of 1943 there were about 10,000 partisans; the figure had trebled by spring 1944, and by early summer it reached 80,000. At the beginning of 1945 there were about 130,000 partisans. Forty to fifty per cent of the fighters belonged to Communist formations—the *Garibaldi* brigades. Another 30 per cent of the partisans were enrolled in the Justice and Liberty (*Giustizia e Libertà*, or 'GL') brigades of the Action Party, with leaders from the professional classes. The remaining insurgents were usually Socialists in the *Matteotti* Brigades, Liberals, or Catholics, known as 'Green Flames'. In several regions there were also self-proclaimed non-political formations—the *Autonomi*—which were created by regular army officers who remained true to their oath of loyalty to the King. On 13 October 1943 the Royalist government in the south declared war on Germany, a move that won Italy the status of co-belligerent with the Allies.

The Allied military intelligence agencies provided a bridge to the Resistance. The British Special Operations Executive (SOE) was created on 19 July 1940 'to coordinate all action by way of subversion and sabotage against the enemy overseas'. The organisation's first ministerial head, Hugh Dalton, said:

> 'Sabotage' was a simple idea. It meant smashing things up. 'Subversion' was a more complex conception. It meant the weakening, by whatever covert means, of the enemy's will and power to make war, and the strengthening of the will and power of his opponents, including in particular, guerrilla and resistance movements.[1]

The Labour politician had served as a lieutenant in the Royal Garrison Artillery of the British Army on the Italian front during the First World War. He was awarded the Italian Bronze Medal for Military Valour in recognition of his contempt for danger during the retreat from Caporetto. His memoir, *With British Guns in Italy, A Tribute to Italian Achievement*, is dedicated to 'the high cause of Anglo-Italian friendship and understanding.'[2]

The United States Office of Strategic Services (OSS) was founded on 13 June 1942 for the collection of intelligence, espionage, counter-espionage, psychological operations and guerrilla warfare.

Subversive forces such as SOE and the Special Operations (SO) branch of the OSS sabotaged enemy communications, roads, railways and telephone lines. Their secondary mission was to aid in the organisation, training, operations and supply of resistance groups. The troops worked undercover and usually wore civilian clothing.

Raiding forces such as the British Special Air Service (SAS) and the American Operational Groups (OGs) of the OSS destroyed enemy installations and means of communication. The troops were trained in airborne and amphibious operations, usually working in groups of two to fifteen men, wearing uniforms, with specific objectives to attack.

Allied air forces provided the planes and crews to transport agents, deliver weapons and supplies, evacuate personnel, and drop propaganda leaflets. The covert operations were coordinated by the British SOE and the American OSS. Flights were also made for the British SAS and the Secret Intelligence Service (SIS) under its cover name of the Inter-Services Liaison Department; flights for escape and evasion services were undertaken for the British MI9 (under the cover name of IS9) and the American MIS-X; and flights were also made for the joint Psychological Warfare Board (PWB).

The dramatic political and military changes in Italy during the second half of 1943 forced the people to decide whether to accept or reject the German occupation and the return of Fascism. The consequent clandestine struggle of the partisans was one of the heroic achievements of the Second World War. The participation of the Allies was a crucial factor in the success of the unconventional war, and linked the Resistance with the main campaign. The story is full of fascinating characters and meaningful events.

2

Prisoner Partisans

Several thousand Allied servicemen served with the partisan forces. Most of the volunteers had fled prisoner of war camps after the Italian Armistice and Surrender of September 1943. As well as the obvious dangers, the men faced losing the protection afforded to them under International Law by the 1929 Geneva Convention Relative to the Treatment of Prisoners of War.

Allied figures from the summer had recorded 79,533 prisoners of war in Italy, made up of 42,194 Britons, 26,126 from other Commonwealth countries, 9,903 European allies (Free French, Greeks, Russians and Yugoslavs) and 1,310 from the United States. Most of the men were taken prisoner during the great tank battles in the North African desert from 1940 to 1943, especially in 1942 in Cyrenaica, the eastern province of the Italian colony of Libya. The rest of the captives were airmen and ship and submarine crews from across the Mediterranean Theatre.

In August 1943 the British War Office identified fifty-two main prisoner of war camps in Italy, using the prefix 'PG' and listing their official number.[1] The size and location of a network of satellite work camps were largely unknown; they had spread rapidly after employment was made compulsory for 'other ranks' in the summer of 1942. There were also eighteen prison hospitals and seven camps for civilian internees.

A message had been sent to the camps in Italy by the British escape and evasion service, MI9, using coded letter or radio messages. What became known as the 'stand fast order' was dated 7 June 1943. It was addressed to the Senior British Officer (SBO) or his Allied equivalent:

In the event of an Allied invasion of Italy, Officers Commanding prison camps will ensure that prisoners of war remain within camp. Authority is granted to all Officers Commanding to take necessary disciplinary action to prevent individual prisoners attempting to rejoin their own units

The third article of the Armistice and Surrender document of 3 September also emphasised:

All prisoners or internees of the United Nations [the official name for the Allies] are to be immediately turned over to the Allied Commander in Chief, and none of these may now or at any time be evacuated to Germany.

The Allied Senior Officers in the camps faced a dangerous dilemma when German occupation became a reality within hours of the announcement of the Italian Armistice and Surrender on the evening of 8 September. In the morning, most read out the 'stand fast order' to their men, but events were moving beyond their control. Instead of the advancing Allied troops on the horizon, there were only Germans.

The reaction of the Italian gaolers to their captives was crucial. Before the Armistice only a handful of Allied servicemen had managed to escape the country, reflecting the fact that once outside their camps they faced an overwhelmingly hostile population. However, on 6 September 1943 the Italian War Office had sent this order to their camp commandants:

British POWs—Prevent them falling into German hands. In the event that it is not possible to defend efficiently all the camps, set at liberty all the white prisoners but keep the blacks in prison. Facilitate their escape either to Switzerland or along the Adriatic coast to southern Italy. Labour units in civilian clothes may also be helped, provided they are away from the German line of retreat. At the opportune moment the freed prisoners should be given reserve rations and directions as to which route they should follow.

The Italian officers in many main camps did attempt to carry out the order, while in most work camps the guards simply decided to return home as quickly as possible and the prisoners were left to their own devices. As a result, almost 50,000 Allied prisoners of war were able to flee into the Italian countryside—the greatest mass escape in history.

At the end of hostilities, MI9 published a report on British Commonwealth and United States escapers and evaders across the theatres in which the secret service operated.[2] We can deduce for Italy:

British Commonwealth Escapers:

PoWs in Italy at the time of the Armistice	70,000
Escaped to Switzerland	4,852
Escaped to Allied lines	11,776
Total	16,628
Transferred to Germany	53,372

American Escapers:

Escaped to Switzerland	24
Escaped to Allied lines	1,052
Total	1,076

British Commonwealth Evaders:

Escaped to Switzerland	64
Escaped to Allied lines	134
Total	198

American Evaders:

Escaped to Switzerland	203
Escaped to Allied lines	2,414
Total	2,617

The successful return of escapers and evaders was partly the result of work by the dedicated secret services, the British MI9 and the United States MIS-X. In Italy, they worked together under the banner of N Section of 'A' Force, the deception and escape organisation of Allied Forces Headquarters. The wartime head of MI9, Brigadier Norman Crockatt, said that it can be reasonably claimed that 90 per cent of Commonwealth evaders and 33 per cent of escapers were brought out as a result of its organisation and activities. Almost two in three of the men who returned home were from Italy. After taking into account official rescue work, about a tenth of evaders and two-thirds of escapers would have been saved by nationals of the Fascist state.

In his history of the Second World War, wartime British Prime Minister Winston S. Churchill wrote:

> Mussolini's bid for a Fascist revival plunged Italy into the horrors of civil war. In the weeks following the September armistice officers and men of the Italian Army stationed in German-occupied northern Italy and patriots from the town and countryside began to form partisan units and to operate against the Germans and against their compatriots who still adhered to the *Duce*. Contacts were made with the Allied armies south of Rome and with the Badoglio Government. In these months the network of Italian resistance to the German occupation was created in a cruel atmosphere of civil strife, assassinations and executions. The insurgent movement in central and northern Italy, here as elsewhere in occupied Europe, convulsed all classes of the people.

Not the least of their achievements was the succour and support given to our prisoners of war trapped by the armistice in camps in northern Italy. Out of about eighty thousand of these men, conspicuously clothed in battle dress, and in the main with little knowledge of the language or geography of the country, at least ten thousand, mostly helped by the local population with civilian clothes, were guided to safety thanks to the risks taken by members of the Italian Resistance and the simple people of the countryside. [3]

Contact between the Allies and the Resistance began in the winter of 1943 and was given added urgency by the presence of the thousands of escaped prisoners of war in the countryside. The Milan Liberation Committee set up the *Ufficio Assistenza Prigionieri di Guerra Alleati* (the Assistance Service for Allied Prisoners of War) within two weeks of the announcement of the Armistice, telling the Allies that it felt honour-bound to do so 'from a humanitarian point of view and for the good name of this country'. Support networks spread throughout occupied Italy and reinforced the efforts of the official British and American search and rescue agencies and the spontaneous gestures of small groups and individuals.

Foreign nationals created their own partisan units in some areas. A Czechoslovak detachment numbering 600 men fought alongside rebels in the Piedmont valleys during the summer and autumn of 1944, before they crossed the Alps to join the French campaign. A battalion known as the *Freies Deutschland*, composed of Austrian, German and Czechoslovak deserters from the *Wehrmacht,* operated with the *Garibaldi* brigades on the border with Austria from the summer of 1944 till the end of the war. A partisan band in Umbria primarily made up of Yugoslavs cooperated closely with the Italian *Gramsci* Brigade until the region was liberated in the summer of 1944. Soviet escapers in Emilia formed several units that were famous for their military prowess, discipline and good relations with other partisans and the civilian population.

However, most of the foreign volunteers in the partisan brigades fought individually or in small groups. In a survey covering Emilia-Romagna, Guerrino Franzini revealed that there were at least 1,401 foreign partisans operating in the region. [4] They suffered a high rate of attrition, with 134 fatalities—almost 10 per cent of the total. The men were from seventeen or more nations. The figures are as follows: Soviets 1,032; Germans and Austrians 155; Yugoslavs 70; Poles 49; French 23; Czechoslovaks 23; Britons 14; Greeks 8; Dutch 7; Americans 2; New Zealanders 2; Luxembourgers 2; Turks 2; Australians 1; Danes 1; Swiss 1; and nationality unknown 9. The Germans and Austrians were mainly deserters from the *Wehrmacht* during the last months of the war. The foreign partisans were not distributed evenly over the eight provinces. There were 443 in Parma; 295 in Piacenza; 201 in Reggio; 195 in Modena; 172 in Bologna (a partial figure); and only 95 between the three easterly provinces of Ferrara, Forli and Ravenna.

The author noted that most foreigners were repatriated following the demobilisation of the partisan formations after the ceasefire on 2 May 1945. As a result, their status as combatants was not validated by any screening commission. This was in contrast to their colleagues from Italy, where a decree of 21 August 1945 set up regional committees and basically defined a 'fighting partisan' as someone who had served for at least three months in one of the recognised armed formations.

However, leading foreign protagonists were honoured with awards, including the Italian Gold or Silver Medal for Military Valour, the United States Bronze Star, and other foreign decorations. The Italian Ministry of Defence also issued certificates to foreigners recording their service in the Corps of the Volunteers for Liberty, the fighting forces of the National Liberation Committee in the north. Additionally, similar documents were issued by the Communist *Garibaldi* brigades and other partisan formations.

In turn, the Allies awarded Italian partisans the *Certificato al Patriota* (or the 'Patriots' Certificate'). It is known popularly as the *Brevetto Alexander*, as it is signed (in facsimile) by the Field Marshal. He presented the first certificate in person to an Italian credited with having saved his life and that of Winston Churchill on 26 August 1944. The British Prime Minister was in Italy to supervise the launch of Operation Olive, the attack of the 8th Army on the Gothic Line. Shortly before the pair were due to travel along the main road in the Saltara area of the Metauro Valley, south of Pesaro, Nello Iacchini came upon an isolated German armed with a mortar. The partisan disarmed the soldier and handed him over to Canadian troops accompanying the leaders.

The first historian of the Italian Resistance was not only a partisan but also partly of British descent and an agent of its subversion and sabotage agency, the Special Operations Executive. Roberto Battaglia, born in Rome, was an army officer during Italy's wars in Africa, an art historian, and a member of the Action Party. He fought in the Justice and Liberty brigades in Umbria, and once the region was liberated he was parachuted by SOE to northern Tuscany in June 1944. Roberto became political commissar to the Lunese *Garibaldi* Division. Its commander was a British escaped prisoner of war from PG 29 Veano—Major Anthony 'Tony' Oldham MC, of the Indian Army. The division carried out fifty sabotage operations, causing 1,000 enemy casualties, and for four days even occupied the City of Carrara. However, on 27 November a massive roundup was unleashed and the formation splintered. Roberto and Tony were among hundreds of partisans forced to retreat across the Gothic Line. On the recommendation of the Allies, Roberto was awarded the Italian Silver Medal for Military Valour. Tony received the British Distinguished Service Order and remained in Italy to marry one of his wartime helpers.

In the preface to his book *The Story of the Italian Resistance,* Roberto wrote of the lasting ties that were created by fighting together in the mountains:

It is true that during the War of Liberation the relations between the Allies and the partisans were fraught with difficulties, difficulties that were the result of political differences ... I and my fellow countrymen who rose up in arms and fought to free themselves from the Nazi yoke will never forget the debt of gratitude we owe to the Allies. Political disagreements and misunderstandings can go by the board. We remember the fact that British officers and men fought side by side with us against the common enemy and for the same cause: the cause of freedom.[5]

How the opponents of the Nazis and Fascists coalesced into a victorious force is the topic of the next chapter.

3

The Allies and the Resistance

At 7.42 p.m. on 8 September 1943, a music programme on Italian radio was suddenly interrupted by a recorded message from Marshal Pietro Badoglio:

> The Italian Government has asked General Eisenhower, Commander in Chief of the Anglo-American forces, for an armistice. This request has been granted. Consequently, every hostile act towards the Anglo-American forces on the part of the Italian forces must cease in every location. They will, however, respond to possible attacks from any other quarter.

As German troops secured Rome, the next day the leaders of the banned anti-Fascist parties gathered at the premises of the Einaudi publishers on Via Adda. They voted to form the National Liberation Committee, or the '*Comitato di Liberazione Nazionale*'. Six groups were represented at the gathering— Actionists, Christian Democrats, Communists, Democrats, Liberals and Socialists. Ivanoe Bonomi, who had briefly been prime minister before Mussolini's seizure of power, was elected president.

At the end of the meeting the members passed a resolution:

> At the moment in which Nazism tries to restore its Fascist ally in Rome and Italy, the anti-Fascist parties have united in the National Liberation Committee, CLN, to call on the Italians to resist and to ensure that the country returns to the place it deserves among the ranks of free nations.

On 16 October the CLN issued its manifesto:

1. To assume the constitutional powers of the state.
2. To carry on the war alongside the Allies.
3. To consult the people on the future form of government at the end of hostilities.

Satellite committees were gradually created across the regions and provinces of occupied Italy. Each CLN had its own leaders, underground press and control over irregular forces—the partisans. In turn, the fighters were dependent upon the politicians in the towns for money, supplies and forged papers.

The lead was taken by the Milan CLN. They sent Alberto Damiani to meet John McCaffery, the head of SOE Switzerland, at the end of October. Leo Valiani also came from the south to contact the CLN. He had been recruited by SOE in Mexico and became one of their most influential operatives. On 3 November, Valiani and his Action Party colleague, Ferruccio Parri, met John McCaffery and Allen Dulles of OSS near Lugano. Parri, a future prime minister, was a founder member of the Action Party in 1942 and leader of its partisan formations. He favoured *grossa guerra* (all-out war), but found that the Allies' aims were more limited. They set four priorities for the Resistance— sabotage, intelligence, aid to Allied escapers, and, with many reservations, guerrilla warfare. The movement would be subject to Allied orders and above all would have to prepare for the last phase of the battle, when its role would be to open the way for the advancing troops.

The Italians were promised money and supplies. The sum of 50 million lire was sent, but the British Foreign Office intervened to ensure that only a handful of agents and limited supplies were parachuted. The first drop on 23 December provided equipment for just thirty men. The CLN complained bitterly, saying that the Allies were defaulting on their promises and only wanted random acts of sabotage.

The British and American governments believed that the monarchy and its administration under Marshal Badoglio were the only legitimate sources of power; the Resistance was viewed as republican, left-wing and Communist. In Churchill's words to President Roosevelt in February 1944:

> The present regime is the lawful Government of Italy, with whom we have concluded an armistice, in consequence of which the Italian Navy came over, and, with some of the Italian Army and Air Force, are fighting on our side. This Italian Government will obey our directions far more than any other that we may laboriously constitute.[1]

The War Office also disliked irregulars and did not want to hear talk of politics or discussions on the future of the country. A proper professional soldier had to exclude such considerations.

In January 1944 the Milan CLN claimed the right to direct resistance across the north, becoming the central liberation committee for German-occupied Italy—the *CLN Alta Italia* or CLNAI. The president was the independent banker Alfredo Pizzoni. Members were drawn from five parties—Liberals, Socialists, Actionists, Communists and Christian Democrats. After the landings at Anzio on the 22nd, the more moderate Rome CLN spoke of the CLNAI as the 'extraordinary government' of the north and called on it to 'promote and lead popular participation in the liberation struggle in a climate of unity between the anti-Fascist forces'.

The first statement of the CLNAI was strongly anti-monarchist, asserting: 'There will be no place tomorrow among us for a reactionary regime'. The committee informed the Allies that they intended to take territory back from the Germans and wanted to be treated as the rightful government, independent of the Royalist administration in the south. At a congress of anti-Fascist parties held in the liberated territory at Bari, the left-wingers, led by the CLN, were unanimous in demanding the King's immediate abdication.

The bridging of the gap between anti-Fascists in the north and south came from an unexpected source—the Communist leader Palmiro Togliatti. He had been exiled for life by the Fascists and had already spent eighteen years abroad, but in March 1944 he was able to return from Moscow to southern Italy. Togliatti was aware that there was no possibility of revolution in a country emerging from twenty years of Fascism and occupied by the Allies, so he announced the abandonment of revolutionary action in favour of national unity, progressive democracy and a permanent coalition of the popular parties.

The Communist leader told a meeting of his National Council in Naples:

> It is impossible to give any guarantee of freedom to the Italian people until the Nazis have been driven from our native soil. We must, therefore, redouble our war effort in order to liberate our country. Let us, then, form a national government. In doing so we shall be taking an immense step forward.

The anti-Fascist parties adopted a plan whereby King Victor Emmanuel would hand over his powers to his son, Crown Prince Umberto, who would be created Lieutenant-General on the day the Allies entered Rome. A coalition government was formed under Marshal Badoglio on 24 April. Following the liberation of the capital on 4 June, the CLN president, Ivanoe Bonomi, replaced the Marshal as leader of a new government in Rome. The principle of national coalition was fulfilled in the ministry, which declared itself to be the expression of the Committee of National Liberation.

The CLNAI approved the formation of the new government, and in the summer there was a noticeable increase in Allied support for the Resistance. Two days after the liberation of Rome, in his first message to the partisans, General Alexander called on them to 'rise in force against the common enemy … hitting them by every means'. The liberation of much of central Italy (and of southern France in August) encouraged hopes of a final Allied victory.

On 10 June 1944 the military committee of the CLNAI was transformed into the central military command for occupied Italy under the banner of the

Corps of Volunteers for Liberty—the *Corpo Volontari della Libertà*, or CVL. The joint leaders were the commander of the *Garibaldi* brigades, Luigi Longo, and the commander of the GL brigades, Ferruccio Parri. Longo was Inspector General to the International brigades during the Spanish Civil War, and Parri had been a staff officer in the Italian Army in the First World War. The creation of the CVL was a military necessity, but it was also inspired by the wish to have one body to deal with the Italian government and AFHQ.

The concept of a military committee affiliated to the CLN but working independently of it was extended across occupied Italy. A vertical chain of command ran from the central CVL committee to regional and provincial bodies. They in turn directed divisions (the operational units), which were composed of two or more brigades (the tactical formations). The days of isolated partisan bands were over. A report from the Resistance to AFHQ spoke of 70,000 partisans; they claimed that this figure could be doubled if they were given adequate money and proper weapons and supplies. The first Allied military and political liaison missions arrived behind enemy lines and support increased. The rebels created liberated zones in Piedmont, Lombardy, Liguria, Emilia and the Veneto. By the end of the summer, there were eighteen of these 'partisan republics'. Several of them had sizeable populations—notably Montefiorino with 50,000, Ossola with 70,000 and Carnia with 150,000.

These developments presented major problems for the Allies. The Italians obviously did not intend to confine themselves to the role of a body of snipers and saboteurs. An SOE officer commented wryly:

> Amid the confusion of aims and methods which inevitably marked this vigorous renaissance of the democratic spirit in Italy, SOE strove, and is still striving, to retain a substantial measure of operational control over its manifestations.

In July 1944 the Allied Control Commission created a Patriots Branch as a result of these concerns. Its main role was to handle relations with the Resistance, with special attention being paid to the final phase of the struggle.

On 25 June the CLNAI had asked for General Raffaele Cadorna to be sent north to become their 'military advisor'. The Piedmontese soldier belonged to Italy's most distinguished military family; he had been a cavalry officer during the First World War, and in September 1943 he had valiantly opposed the German occupation of Rome as commander of the *Ariete* armoured division. He managed to evade capture and became a member of the underground Military Front led by Colonel Montezemolo. On 12 August the General was parachuted into the Val Cavallina, east of Bergamo, in Operation Fairway. He was accompanied by twenty-nine-year-old Italian-speaking SOE officer Major Oliver Churchill MC, wireless operator Sergeant Delle Monache, and customs guard Lieutenant Augusto De Laurentis. It was the General's first parachute drop at age fifty-five. He went to Milan after a week and was joined by Major Churchill and the radio operator on 14 September.

Before leaving for enemy territory, the team had been briefed by Lieutenant-General John Harding on Allied policy concerning supply drops, resistance and liberation. They also received a message of good wishes from General Alexander. The Italian government showed no interest in the mission and the Americans were not consulted—they viewed it as an attempt by SOE to re-establish its domination of special operations in Italy. On 16 March 1944 OSS Secret Intelligence mission Apricot, led by Enzo Boeri, had parachuted north-west of Milan to provide a radio link between the CLNAI and AFHQ. The agents became responsible for leading the partisan intelligence service, and every day they transmitted the committee's official war bulletins, which were passed to AFHQ, the BBC and world media outlets. OSS sent a second mission to liaise with the CLNAI, with the operation being composed of two teams—Chrysler (part of an Operational Group) and Mangosteen (Secret Intelligence). The mission came to grief with the murder of its commander, Major William Hollohan, on the shores of Lake Orta on 6 December 1944. He was allegedly killed by some of his companions, though the case has never been decisively resolved in court.

General Cadorna told the CLNAI that they could rely on money and supplies from the Allies, but that aid would be suspended if operations were impeded by political disagreements. The committee saw the General's role as purely advisory, but the British saw him as the future military commander of the CVL. As a result, a crisis meeting was held at Lugano in October 1944. SOE was represented by Colonel Cecil Roseberry and John McCaffery, while Ferruccio Parri and Leo Valiani spoke for the CLNAI. The Italians agreed to send a delegation south to formalise military relations with the Allies and political links with the Rome government. In a report dated 31 October, the Colonel said: 'The Allies should support the CLNAI while maintaining close liaison to ensure operational control'.

Major Churchill's reports to base showed scepticism over the work of the CVL and preference for the independent formations. On 2 December he was withdrawn as the result of pressure from the CLNAI. Two days later, the CVL announced its compromise command structure: Raffaele Cadorna (Valenti), commandant; Luigi Longo (Gallo or Italo) and Ferruccio Parri (Maurizio), vice commandants; the Socialist Giovanni Battista Stucchi, chief of staff; and the Liberal Mario Argenton and the Christian Democrat Enrico Mattei, staff officers. On 21 February 1945 General Cadorna was dismissed by the CLNAI as the result of a policy disagreement. He was reinstated a week later after the intervention of the Allies and the Rome Government.

In a message to the CVL on 6 September 1944, General Alexander said:

> The total defeat of the Germans, to which you have contributed with such great success, is now in sight ... continue the attack on military objectives,

means of communication and isolated groups of Germans in retreat. Thank you for all your help.

On the 18th, the CVL issued instructions to the formations to go on the offensive. The 8th Army made some progress in the eastern sector, with tactical support being provided by SOE and the partisans. Rimini was taken on 21 September, and Ravenna on 4 December in an operation described by Roberto Battaglia as 'the finest example of collaboration between the patriots and the Allies in the entire history of the Resistance'. The offensive involved Arrigo Boldrini's 28th *Garibaldi* Brigade, Popski's Private Army and regular Canadian forces. The partisans entered the line under the command of the British V Corps and in February 1945 became a unit of the Italian Royal Army.

However, the Allied assault on the Gothic Line eventually ground to a halt. The Germans and Fascists brought up five divisions and auxiliary formations to take on the partisans; the guerrillas were forced to take up defensive positions in the vain hope of preventing the liberated zones from being overrun.

On 13 November, General Alexander issued his controversial declaration to the Resistance. In a radio message the partisans were told that the present phase of the campaign was over, and they were to prepare to face a new enemy—the winter. As a result, he told the fighters, they should:

1. Cease for the present from engaging in any large-scale operations.
2. Conserve all stores of ammunition, and await further orders.
3. Listen in whenever possible to the broadcasts of *Italia Combatte* transmitted from Allied HQ in order to keep in touch with any changes that might occur in the situation and to be in readiness to act on new directives.

The proclamation was the responsibility of Alexander's Chief of Staff, Lieutenant-General John Harding. After the war, he related that the decision had been made on purely military grounds:

The military advance had run out of steam by November 1944. The US 5th Army could make no progress in the mountains and the 8th Army were only making limited attacks to improve their position. Alex and I thought if the partisans went on with their operations they would suffer so many casualties that they would not be able to play the part we wanted in the final offensive. We felt that once the main battle front became quiet, the Germans and the Republican Army would have plenty of troops to attack the partisans. We did not consider in detail the psychological effects of the declaration. We had little, if any, contact with SOE in Bern over their role in aiding the partisans.[2]

Allied supplies actually increased after the proclamation. Only five days after it was issued, the SOE Cherokee Mission parachuted to the mainly Communist partisans of Biella in Piedmont. Commandant Major Alastair Macdonald related that on 26 December they received the largest quantity of supplies during the campaign. The cargo comprised: 165 Bren guns; 505 Sten guns; 565 rifles; 5,725 Pigna hand grenades; 85 infantry mortars; and 80 Piat anti-tank grenade launchers, as well as ammunition, explosives, fuses and detonators. British records confirm that there was a steady rise in the tonnage of supplies dropped by Allied aircraft from the start of 1944. The figures for each quarter are 92 tons, 398 tons, 650 tons, 780 tons, and 1,669 tons in the first quarter of 1945 (second, incomplete quarter, 875 tons).

On 2 December 1944, the CLNAI gave its response to the Alexander Proclamation in a document drafted by the Communist Luigi Longo. It stated:

> The partisan war is not, on the part of the Italian people and the patriots who have taken up arms a mere whim, an idle caprice to be refrained from at will. It arose from the vital necessity of defending our material, moral and social heritage. This is the supreme cause for which we have been fighting and must continue to fight day after day. It was and is the duty of every patriot to participate in this war in order that he may retain his individual freedom, his right to live. The war must go on. There must be no relaxation, no weakening. On the contrary, the struggle must be intensified, the armed forces engaged in it greatly increased. We cannot, indeed, we must not, consider any suggestion calculated to deflect us from our purpose: that of widening the sphere of our activities, bringing still larger numbers into the field, and fighting on with an ever growing resolution and will to win.

Though intended to prevent loss of life, the Alexander Proclamation was a great setback for the Resistance and a tonic for the Germans and Republicans. With the guarantee that they would not be liable to suffer a major attack over the winter, they unleashed a series of offensives in the mountains. The troops adopted the tactic of the *rastrellamento* ('roundup'). Armoured columns penetrated the valleys with supporting infantry deployed on the hills, while further units scoured the secondary valleys. The free zones were overrun and savage reprisals were taken against civilians. At the same time, there was increased police activity in the cities. In a few months the military commands of Liguria, Lombardy, Piedmont and the Veneto were arrested.

On 14 November, the day after the Alexander proclamation was issued to the partisans, the CLNAI mission left for Rome. It was led by the president, Alfredo Pizzoni. He was supported by Ferruccio Parri, Giancarlo Pajetta, who was Longo's deputy, and—at the insistence of the Allies—Royalist lieutenant and British agent Edgardo Sogno. The Resistance leaders were brought south by SOE and the OSS.

After prolonged negotiations, a document that became known as the 'Rome Protocols' was signed at the Grand Hotel on 7 December by General Maitland Wilson for the Allies and the four Resistance leaders for the CLNAI. The CVL agreed to carry out the instructions of the Allied Commander in Chief, Field Marshal Alexander (newly promoted on 5 December, effective from the previous 4 June), and protect the north against a scorched-earth policy from the enemy. The CLNAI would nominate a military commander acceptable to the Allies; the choice had already fallen on General Cadorna. The CLNAI undertook that they would maintain law and order during and immediately after the liberation, before handing over their powers to the Allied Military Government. The partisan formations would be disbanded and their weapons surrendered. Finally, Allied missions would be consulted on all matters relating to armed resistance, anti-scorch and the maintenance of order.

The Allies agreed to pay a subsidy of 160 million lire per month to the Resistance. The sum was drawn from money donated by the Italian government as their contribution to the war effort. Alfredo Pizzoni became responsible for the transfer of the funds and their distribution in the north. Only 40 per cent of the subsidy was allocated to the *Garibaldi* brigades, while the other partisan groups received 60 per cent.

On 26 December the new Bonomi Government (now composed of just three parties—the Christian Democrats, Communists and Liberals) also reluctantly signed up to the agreement. It delegated the CLNAI to represent it in the struggle in occupied Italy. In turn, the CLNAI accepted the Italian government as the legitimate authority in the rest of Italy.

On 2 January 1945, the GL partisan leader Ferruccio Parri was captured when arriving at his flat in Milan after returning from his journey to meet the Allies and conclude the Rome Protocols. His colleague, Lieutenant Sogno, attempted to rescue him from the SS Headquarters in the Hotel Regina. The lieutenant entered the building from an adjacent roof and through a skylight. He had three companions—including Stefano Porta, who was later arrested by the British during Operation Boykin. All wore SS uniforms. They were challenged by guards in the hall and arrested. The captives were beaten, interrogated and imprisoned, though Porta managed to escape. Ferruccio Parri was moved to a more secure prison in Verona.

On 14 January 1945 the new head of 15th Army Group, US General Mark Clark, issued an inspiring message to the Resistance:

As a combatant with the Fifth Army I have seen the way in which the Italian patriots have carried out their duty. I have noted the difficult conditions in which they have operated. You can be certain that under my command you will receive the maximum support possible, and for my part I am sure that you will continue to contribute to the common goal of expelling the aggressor from Italian soil.

Only nine days later, AFHQ signalled to the partisans: 'The bad weather has ended. Offensive operations will start again'. However, despite the carefully drafted agreements in the Rome Protocols, the Allies became increasingly uneasy as the final offensive loomed. The British Foreign Office continued to highlight the Communist menace and insisted that AFHQ should adopt a new attitude towards the partisans. However, the implementation of the military terms of the Rome Protocols was the responsibility of SOE and OSS, which went far beyond their core role of liaison. They adopted a more trusting attitude towards the partisans and their demand for supplies and sent several missions to Communist formations during this period.

At the beginning of February, the commandant of the SS in Italy, General Karl Wolff, had started secret talks with Allen Dulles for the surrender of German forces in Italy—without informing the Fascists. As a sign of good faith, Wolff was asked for the liberation of Ferruccio Parri and American agent Antonio Usmiani. The pair were taken to Switzerland and handed over to Dulles on 8 March.

Meanwhile, General Cadorna, Leo Valiani and Ferruccio Parri met Allied representatives in Switzerland to discuss the imminent assault on the Gothic Line and actions to be taken on the liberation. General Cadorna and Ferruccio Parri came south at the beginning of April and took part in talks with 15th Army Group and SOE and OSS on the role the CLNAI would play in the final phase of military operations. On 6 April, the day after the Allied offensive began in the west, the partisan leaders left for Milan and the final battle.

The democratic future of Italy was assured, owing to the unity of the resistance and the support of the Allies. In a speech on the constitution given to students in Milan in 1955, the jurist Piero Calamandrei said:

> If you wish to go on a pilgrimage to the place where our constitution was born, go to the mountains where the partisans fell, to the jails where they were imprisoned, to the fields where they were hanged. Wherever an Italian has died with the aim of redeeming freedom and dignity, go there young man, with the thought that this is where our constitution was born.

One of the most popular places of pilgrimage is the farmhouse of Campi Rossi at Gattatico, which was the wartime home of the Cervi family. Their story, and that of the escaped Allied prisoners of war they helped, is the subject of the next two chapters.

4

The Cervi Band

In the summer of 1943, captive Red Army soldier Anatolij Tarasov from Leningrad was deployed in laying telephone and telegraph lines as an auxiliary for the German Army in the countryside of Reggio Emilia. Born in 1921, he became an infantryman in 1940 and was captured by the Germans during their invasion of the Soviet Union. Anatolij escaped on the 1943 Armistice, together with fellow Russian Victor Pirogov (Danilo), while the Germans were burning some of the items looted from Italian garrisons during their takeover.

In the morning, the escapers approached a group of Italians in the fields, but because of their blonde appearance and hesitant manner they were treated with suspicion. The pair decided to walk along the Via Emilia. They saw an oncoming German patrol and took refuge in a roadside inn. The troops came in too, but their only interest was in drinking and in making a nusiance of themselves with a young woman. Once the soldiers had driven off, the pair managed to explain to the innkeeper that they were Russian escapers. He told them that Germans had killed one of his relatives and deported another to Germany. 'Now we have the same enemies to fight,' he said, and found them temporary accommodation in the barn of a nearby farmer.

At around midday, the escapers were visited by two Italians. One was an elderly anti-Fascist, and the other was Walter Corradini, a tall and thin office worker in his early thirties. He said that in the evening they would be billeted with trusted comrades and offered them a pistol, which Victor accepted. Corradini called for him first. A farmer came for Anatolij. He was Aldo Cervi (Gino), future organiser of the first partisan detachment. He was slightly below average height, stocky, with a calm and open face, strong hands, and a battered pair of shoes that were splashed with dung.

Anatolij was given a bicycle and cap and followed Aldo along a gravel road that wound through a pleasant landscape of fields and water courses, scattered with pretty, white-painted farms. They finally reached the Cervi homestead of Campi Rossi at Gattatico. It was a large, stone building surrounded by fields, which were crossed by rows of vines and elms. A big door divided the farmhouse in two; on one side were the living quarters and the cellar, and on the other was the cattleshed, with a barn above. The building housed three generations of the Cervi family: the father and mother, Alcide, and Genoveffa Cocconi; seven sons, aged between twenty-two and forty-two—Ettore, Ovidio, Agostino, Ferdinando, Aldo, Antenore and Gelindo; four wives; and ten children. There were also several partisans and escaped prisoners of war. Two married daughters, Rina and Diomira, lived locally with their husbands' families.

The eldest brother, Gelindo, explained that the Cervis had been poor sharecroppers until they rented Campi Rossi in 1934. They had levelled the land and devised a new system of irrigation. At first the neighbours were sceptical about the innovations, but they gradually began to adopt them too. In 1939 Aldo had driven a new Landini tractor back from Reggio—one of the first in the area—and placed a globe on the top as a sign of the infinite possibilities ahead.

The family had engaged in the political struggle ever since 1932, when Aldo returned from a term of incarceration in the military prison at Gaeta. He had been called up for national service three years earlier and served at Conegliano; however, when on sentry duty at a powder magazine, he had fired at an officer who had not given a password. The gaol was full of anti-Fascists, and especially Communists. They taught Aldo that that Fascism suppressed the best impulses of the Italian people and had to be fought. Aldo passed on these ideas to his brothers, and they began to frequent libraries and to read books on agriculture, politics and economics. The family even founded their own library in the nearby commune of Campegine, with the intention of educating and radicalising the local populace.

At the end of 1941 the underground Communist Party sent a representative to liaise with the Cervis. Lucia Sarzi, twenty years old, was an actress in her family's travelling theatre company. They had moved to Parma when Italy entered the war in June 1940, and her performances of classic roles gave her audiences thoughts of the freedom that they were denied under the dictatorship. Lucia contacted the party and was given the task of reviving the scattered ranks of militants in the neighbouring province of Reggio. Her younger brother, Otello, was in enforced exile in Calabria as a political dissident. Through Lucia, the Cervis gained a direct link to conspirators in the towns and cities.

Aldo read out the text of underground newspapers to his neighbours and wrote his own leaflets, which Gelindo and Lucia helped him distribute in Mantua. From Radio Moscow they learned of the German surrender at Stalingrad and that of Rommel's forces in North Africa. Lucia produced pamphlets praising the Red Army and setting out ways to sabotage the war effort. The brothers scattered the leaflets from the balconies of cinemas onto the stalls, and at night they cycled to Reggio and fixed them on walls. At the beginning of 1943, four members of the family spent a snowy night demolishing a high-tension electric pylon near the farm.

When the fall of Mussolini and the Fascist regime was announced on 25 July, the Cervis sang and danced in the courtyard of their farm. In the morning they led a group of peasants in a march on the San Tommaso gaol in Reggio; the doors were thrown open and the political detainees were released. The next day, together with their neighbours, the family prepared a meal of *pastaciutta* for the inhabitants of Campegine, and carried it to the central square in their vehicles. Even the police joined in the festival to celebrate the end of Fascism. However, the euphoria was brief. Aldo pointed to Marshal Badoglio's statement, 'The war will go on alongside our German ally.' On 28 July, workers emerging from their factories in Reggio for a peace demonstration were fired on by soldiers. There were nine fatalities.

After the announcement of the Armistice on the evening of 8 September, the Germans occupied the city and overwhelmed the Italian troops. Most were marched to the railway station for deportation to Germany; any who managed to escape were hidden by civilians, who also helped escaped Allied prisoners of war. On 28 September a provincial resistance organisation, the CLN, was created in the city by members of the Action Party, Catholics, Communists and Socialists.

Anatolij went to help Ettore cut and load grass, with Gelindo to spray the vines, with Aldo to collect the grapes, and with Ferdinando to place the fruit in vats to create young wine. One day, Ettore invited the Russian to the cinema in the village of Caprara. He was given a pistol to carry. During the performance, Ettore scattered leaflets from the balcony. Two days later, Anatolij went to the cinema with Aldo. On the way back they stopped at a peasant's house, and Aldo brought out two young men to meet Anatolij. One was an escaped South African prisoner of war known as 'Jeppy' (his real name was John Peter de Freitas). His companion was an artistic Italian called Dante Castellucci. He was from Calabria, but for many years he had studied and worked in France. Dante was called up on the eve of Italy's entry in the war and wounded on the Russian front in 1942. He had previously met Otello Sarzi, and, after convalescing, joined the family's travelling theatre company, playing the violin and guitar and sharing in their anti-Fascist activities.

Walter Corradini found Anatolij new lodgings with a peasant just outside Reggio. The man said that he was not a Communist, but had given him sanctuary because Walter was a good and honest man and a fighter for peasant rights. Anatolij met Lucia Sarzi for the first time. He recalled that she was not very tall and had a pleasant, oval face. Lucia had printed the leaflets that

Ettore distributed in the cinema. She welcomed Anatolij as the representative of the Soviet Union, the first socialist state in the world.

The Cervis believed that as the royal family and the government had fled south, the only hope for the salvation of Italy lay in what the people could do for themselves. With their own brand of romantic Communism, the family's response was instinctive and immediate. They decided to turn their house into a centre of resistance, with the ultimate aim of creating a partisan group that could survive in the mountains to the south.

The farm became a clearing house for disbanded Italian soldiers and escaped Allied prisoners of war. The Cervis exchanged the troops' weapons for peasant clothes and turned the barns into arsenals. Alcide Cervi recalled that he sheltered more than eighty prisoners in his house. The local camp was PG 73 Carpi, which was housed in new brick-built barracks in the hamlet of Fossoli, 4 miles north of Modena. On 30 June the camp had held 4,793 prisoners of war, including Britons, Australians, Indians, New Zealanders and South Africans. The men came in tattered clothes and were sometimes infested with lice, but they went away clean, clothed and fattened. The children scoured the area to obtain civilian clothing for the escapers, and the womenfolk often worked until 1 a.m. to adapt the garments.

One day a *staffetta* (a female courier) rushed in and said that an American airman had dropped by parachute in the countryside. They found him losing blood from a wound in his leg. He feared that they were Fascists, but beamed when they said, '*Partigiani*.' They took him home in the car. The airman kissed Genoveffa like his mother when he saw the comfortable and clean bed waiting for him. The sons put his leg in a splint; Ferdinando got a nurse to call and regularly dressed the wound himself. Alcide recalled that they served the American boiled chicken for dinner, but he surprised them all by spitting out the skin. The meat was precious to the family. It had to be bought in, as they only had laying hens left.

The airman's condition improved each day. He asked the women in the kitchen the names of various items in Italian and put the words together; they had many amusing conversations. A Russian who was also learning the language came to speak some words of English, and the airman some words of Russian. After supper one evening, the prisoners began to sing songs from their various countries. They ended with the Communist *Internationale*—all sung in their own languages, but with one voice.

The Cervi family were also supplying rebels in the mountains. Gelindo and Antenore did the butchery and preserved the meat in brine. Ferdinando looked after an apiary and provided kilos of honey. The women made bread. Two teams of prisoners helped out; the Britons and South Africans prepared and cooked pasta, and the Russians made butter. The milk supply was diverted to butter production for forty days after the veterinary inspector was tricked into certifying that the cows were suffering from foot and mouth disease and the herd was isolated. The Russians were joined by the other prisoners in producing the butter.

Some of the servicemen chose to attempt to rejoin Allied forces. Groups of escapers would depart into the night on bicycles obtained by the family. The men were provided with money and with rations and equipment for cold and wet weather. Aldo told them to follow the high-tension pylons into the mountains.

Others decided to take up the armed struggle. One fine day at the end of September, a mixed group of about thirty men (Italians and prisoners) left the farm for the distant, blue Apennines. Some travelled on a horse and cart, some on bicycles, and some on foot. Anatolij was among them. He recalled, 'We foreigners, without knowing the language and the customs of the country, would not have been able to do anything by ourselves.'

During the night the group reached the first hills and settled in an empty shepherd's hut. When they awoke they had a nasty surprise; a young man wearing the uniform of the Fascist militia was sitting outside. However, he said that he had deserted the force and that his name was Quarto Camurri. They recovered his discarded musket and breechblock and he joined the group. Their first base was in an abandoned house in chestnut woods surrounding the village of Cervarezza, at the head of the Secchia Valley. They were joined by Otello Sarzi, Lucia's brother, who had escaped confinement and was already in the mountains.

The partisans were in Cervarezza for only five days, as the enemy had learned of their presence. The rebels looted a hut used by the Fascists and climbed to Monte Ventasso (1,727 metres), whose pyramid shape appeared and disappeared among the scudding clouds. They settled in the ancient oratory (or chapel) of Saint Mary Magdalene, which is perched on a desolate rock-strewn plateau on the side of the mountain. The oratory is a one-storey stone building with a gabled facade and a small belfry on the pitched roof. The partisans held meetings in an adjacent room, where Lucia also cooked the last supplies.

One of the Russians, Alexander Aschenco, had a tendency to fraternise with the British and avoid his own compatriots, who noticed that he attended church frequently and dyed his hair black. Aschenco became an informer for the Fascists and denounced many of the helpers who had sheltered him. He was executed by members of one of the Patriotic Action Groups (GAP) in Reggio on 15 November 1944.

One evening the partisans had two unwanted visitors from the provincial Communist hierarchy—Osvaldo Poppi (Davide), a lawyer, who was responsible for coordinating activities in the mountains, and a worker, Gismondo Veroni (Tito). Both had previous military experience. Members of the party had met at Scampalto on 9 September to form a military committee. They were led by Attilio Gombia (Ascanio), who had just returned from Rome with a plan to begin guerrilla warfare. The followers were told to collect weapons and to form sabotage squads and groups of fighters.

Veroni first heard of the Cervis around 20 September; he visited the farm about a week later. Gombia told him that he had received reports that the detachment was operating in the wrong way and that it was imprudent and lacking in discipline. The foreigners in its ranks were also acting towards civilians without the necessary cordiality and understanding to ensure their support. It was decided that Poppi and Veroni would go to Cervarezza to meet Aldo.

Avoiding Fascist garrisons, the delegates cycled into the mountains and contacted Otello Sarzi. In the evening, he took them to a farmhouse where some of the partisans had gathered. Sitting around a table in a small, smoke-filled room were Aldo, Dante, four escaped prisoners of war (two Russians, a Briton and a South African), and a rebel from the village. Poppi and Veroni explained their ideas on the partisan war. They set out the organisation and discipline required of clandestine formations and emphasised the need to behave in an appropriate manner towards the local people.

The pair were frequently interrupted. At one point, the South African took out a large pistol, threw it on the table and said, 'I talk with this.' Aldo just smiled and proceeded to explain that the group intended to garrison and defend Cervarezza, where they had made many friends. The two delegates argued that it would be an impossible task as there were strong Fascist garrisons 9 miles to the north and 6 miles to the south. The priority was for small groups to undertake raids in the plain. The men would be better deployed in attacks on Fascist leaders and in acts of sabotage, and they would be supported in these by the new Patriotic Action Groups (GAP). The suggestion was angrily rejected and Aldo accused the delegates of being weak and opportunistic. Veroni recalled that they also received insults—particularly from Dante and the foreign partisans. The meeting finished late at night and without anything being agreed. Poppi and Veroni cycled back to the plain in the morning and told their comrades what had happened.

On his return from the meeting, Aldo reported that he had told the delegates that the detachment was ready for action. In response, they had been given the task of attacking the police station at Toano; however, the station was far away, and he wanted to discuss it first. Not everyone was disposed to take part, but the plan was finally approved. This is the Fascist report on what took place:

> At 17.45 on 25 October in the Puccione area of the Commune of Toano in this province, two *Carabinieri* from the local station were overtaken by a

covered lorry, painted red, while they were travelling along the provincial highway. Some fifteen civilians armed with muskets and pistols got out and ordered them to surrender their weapons. After having disarmed the *Carabinieri*, the aggressors obliged them to climb into the lorry. They made for Toano. Once there, they overpowered Giacomo Sagri, the only soldier in the barracks, who had opened the door to them. The men seized three muskets, three pistols, ammunition, a Phillips radio apparatus and five pairs of shoes. This done, the unknown aggressors let the *Carabinieri* go free and quickly left in the truck for Villa Minozzo. Arriving at the River Secchia, they abandoned the vehicle and disappeared into the surrounding woods.[1]

Aldo guided his men to Tapignola, in the commune of Villa Minozzo—an arduous journey of seven hours. The young local priest, Don Pasquino Borghi, had already visited the partisans at Sologno. He was able to speak to some of them in English, as he had been a missionary for seven years in the Anglo-Egyptian Sudan. The priest sheltered many Allied prisoners of war and Italian disbanded soldiers in his church. He was also an active member of the Resistance under the alias of 'Albertario'.

Once in Tapignola, the partisans located the rectory. Don Pasquino was clothed in a long, black cassock, which almost impeded his movements. He bowed his head slightly in greeting. The priest had an open and intelligent face and studied his guests carefully from behind the round lenses of his spectacles. His domestic servant was not at all perturbed by the arrival of the partisans; she began to put polenta and wine on the table. He kept saying, 'Poor things, how hungry they are,' and ordered cheese, salami and even more wine. Pointing to one group, the priest whispered in Aldo's ear, 'These must be the Russians. *Santa Madonna*! Truly the ones who the Fascists call the Asiatic barbarians. Now they're here with us. Doesn't this seem strange to you?' Aldo replied that nothing in life was impossible and that the workers had allies in all parts of the world. 'What is most evident is their appetite,' said Don Pasquino, and everyone laughed.

After dinner the priest invited the men to follow him to the church. Someone coughed nervously. 'The Russians don't believe in God,' Don Pasquino said. 'This is a great sin, but we'll disregard that for now.' Their momentary embarrassment disappeared. The priest sat at the organ and began to play sad and solemn choral tunes, with his head raised and tears in his eyes. He trailed his fingers on the final keys and after a brief pause began to play again. With a start the partisans realised that the melody was the old song of the Italian workers, the Red Flag, which they had often heard sung in the Cervi household:

Forward people,
To the rescue,
The Red Flag, the Red Flag.
Forward people,
To the rescue,
The Red Flag will triumph,
The Red Flag will triumph,
The Red Flag will triumph,
The Red Flag will triumph.
Long live Communism and freedom!

5

In Enemy Hands

In October 1943 the creation of the first partisan detachment in the mountains at Cervarezza by the Cervi brothers and escaped Allied prisoners of war led to a tense argument with delegates of the official Communist underground. However, at their suggestion, a few days later the detachment raided the police station at Toano before taking shelter with the partisan priest Don Pasquino Borghi at Tapignola. The rebel leader, Aldo Cervi, would soon reluctantly decide to take the advice of the party's military committee to move back to the plain. The weather was deteriorating and the detachment lacked contacts and supplies.

The band split into small groups. The first to leave at the end of the month was composed of a Russian (Anatolij Tarasov), South Africans John Peter de Freitas ('Jeppy') and Johannes David Bastiaanse ('Basti'), a Briton (Samuel Boone Conley), and the Italian partisan Dante Castellucci. Some of the servicemen also moved north in an attempt to reach neutral Switzerland or south to try and link up with the Allied armies. For the moment, Otello Sarzi and the remaining Italians and Russians remained in the mountains.

Anatolij's group intended to steal a car and to return to Campi Rossi without being noticed. However, the only vehicle they saw was that of the local doctor. The men stayed the night in the barn of a farmer who had sheltered them before. In the morning, he told them to be careful because the people were celebrating the Festival of the Day of the Dead (held on the first or second day of November), and the streets would therefore be crowded.

By noon the partisans had marched down the Enza Valley as far as Ciano. When they reached the outskirts of the town, they began to see fine villas with large grounds. The residents wore party dress and looked at the partisans' torn and dirty clothes with suspicion. The men came across a tempting Alfa Romeo, but they were unable to steal it as several policemen were standing nearby. However, another car drove towards them in Montecchio. The driver soon handed over the keys, enabling the partisans to quickly return to Campi Rossi.

On 6 November the Cervi detachment targeted the *Carabinieri* post in the commune of San Martino in Rio, situated on the plain about 9 miles north-east of Reggio. This is the Fascist account of the raid:

> At around 21.15 on 6 November two individuals [Anatolij and John] arrived at the station on board a Fiat 1100 motor car. One was in German uniform. The other was in plain clothes and acting as interpreter. They told the station commander that a German patrol on the march had fallen into a partisan ambush and asked him for manpower. When he objected at the lack of the necessary written order to validate the request, the soldier claimed that the communication had not been obtained owing to shortage of time and also that he had requisitioned the car to reach the first station. Meanwhile, he left a declaration written in the Ukrainian language. The commandant of the station—Warrant Officer Vitale Tonghini—believing that the request was genuine, ordered a corporal and two soldiers to take their place in the car.
>
> After quarter of an hour the soldiers returned to the station, completely disarmed and saying that the car had stopped just outside town. The two alleged soldiers had got out and were immediately replaced by another four armed individuals who ordered them to hand over their weapons and uniforms and to return to their families.[1]

Some days later, Aldo told his companions that he had heard that another detachment was ready to go to the mountains. They would need the weapons they had hidden there, and it was necessary to return by car to pick them up. There was already snow on the mountains by the time the partisans left the next day, and the peaks were hidden in low cloud. Once they reached Cervarezza, Dante slithered down a path to the house of a comrade who had concealed the weapons. He soon returned and reported that there were Fascists in the village. The group loaded the car quickly and took to the road. They saw the bright lights of lanterns on their right; they heard shouting and then shots. John put his foot down hard on the accelerator and swung around a corner, neglecting to consider that they might fall into a ravine; this desperate measure ensured their escape.

The trip to the mountains made the partisans reflect that for any future visit they needed clothing and footwear more suited to the rigours of winter. This would require considerable expenditure, so the group devised a plan to obtain the necessary funds. One evening, Anatolij and John disguised themselves as British officers and, accompanied by Dante, Johannes and Samuel, drove to the villa of a local magnate. The bogus officers convinced the rich man that they had been parachuted into the area to establish links with the Resistance. They said that they were in straitened circumstances and needed help.

Anatolij and John accompanied the Italian through a little square that led to his studio; the others remained in the villa. A cashier brought a wallet to the owner of the house and he pulled out two packets of banknotes. 'Count it, gentlemen,' he said. 'Now I hope that you'll leave me a receipt.' The cashier prepared paper, pen and ink, and everything was ready for signing. John was about to put the banknotes in his pocket when they heard the roar of an approaching vehicle.

Anatolij and John rushed into the road, followed by their benefactor. The partisans looked where they had parked the car, but all they saw were soldiers jumping down from a lorry. Torches cut a swathe through the darkness. Anatolij fired his pistol and shouted. 'Jeppy! Run, while I stop them!' His friend disappeared around a corner. Anatolij saw the shadows of the Fascists and fired again. He moved sideways, but his feet gave way and he fell into cold water flowing in one of the canals that often emerge on the outskirts of towns. Getting out of the water, Anatolij took his cloak off and ran along the bank of the canal, with bullets whistling above his head. He came to a barbed-wire fence, put his cloak over it, and climbed down to the open fields.

Towards morning, Anatolij found warmth in the straw of a barn. He could not sleep and cautiously climbed down a ladder to the cowshed. A mother and daughter were milking the cows by the light of a carbide lamp. A farmer emerged and said to them calmly, 'We have another guest.' The Russian spent the day with the sharecropper family. They thought that he really was British and told him that one of his compatriots had already left his address with their daughter. Anatolij said that he was sorry that he could not delay. The son acted as his guide, taking him back to the Campegine area—a distance of about 25 miles.

Anatolij stole the bicycle of a young man he met on the road; he apologised, explaining that he was in a hurry to get back to his comrades. The Russian went to the Villa Cavazzoli area, where Walter Corradini lived—about 2 miles north-west of Reggio—but remembered that he was being spied on by the police. Anatolij therefore called upon Ferdinando Ferrari, known as 'Marte'—a greengrocer and member of the Communist military committee who had seen him on several occasions. Ferrari said that it was not prudent to stay with him, as he too was under surveillance, but accompanied Anatolij to the house where he had spent his first night after escaping.

The Russian asked Ferrari if he knew anything about the last night's events. He replied that he had not heard anything and neither had the committee. Reassured that his companions might not have been killed or captured, Anatolij began to explain what had happened. 'You youngsters are in too much of a hurry,' Ferrari said. 'The committee doesn't agree with the way you operate. You're too reckless.'

In the morning, Anatolij returned to Campi Rossi, accompanied by Ferrari. They saw no one in the courtyard and entered the cowshed. The men inside ran forward and embraced Anatolij with fervour; John, Dante, Johannes and Samuel had also managed to escape the Fascist ambush. The magnate's wife had let them out of the house through a secret door when they heard Anatolij's shots. They had fired at the enemy with the aim of recovering the car, but they had been beaten back. Still shooting, they had left the town and taken refuge with peasants who brought them to the Cervi house. John had only recently returned, on his own, carrying all the money.

The Russian (Anatolij), the South Africans (John and Johannes), the Briton (Samuel), and the Italians (Dante Castellucci and Quarto Camurri) were the only guests left at Campi Rossi. Recently there had been thirty prisoners at the farm, but they had gradually moved away in small groups. Lucia told the Cervis that the Liberation Committee wanted the foreigners evacuated; to hide them meant certain execution. Anatolij later wrote: 'A reign of terror had been established.'

Aldo moved the fugitives to a house whose owner was away, but one evening a bespectacled man burst into the kitchen. 'Excuse me if I am disturbing you, dear sirs,' he said sarcastically, raising his hat. 'I know who you are and that my visit is not very welcome. I am aware that you foreigners need asylum, but the government is there for this purpose, so contact them.' The man explained that he was looking after the house for his brother-in-law, a teacher, who was in Rome. 'I do not ask much, only that you leave the house as soon as possible,' he concluded.

The dejected partisans filed out into the road. It was wet and cold, and fog seeped up from the plain. They had to return to Campi Rossi; there was no alternative. Alcide Cervi recalled: 'We looked them in the face, one by one. By now they had become like our sons ... We were not inclined to leave them to their fate or to tell them to fend for themselves.'[2] There were Fascists nearby in Campegine. Aldo and John had come across some more Allied fugitives, but they could not take them in. On the evening of 24 November, the prisoners of war decided to leave in the morning and packed their belongings. The household settled down for a night of peaceful sleep.

Just before dawn, the residents were woken by a series of gunshots. They rushed to the windows. Rain lashed the sills and cattle bellowed in the shed, but no one could be seen. Then a voice rang out.

'Cervis, surrender!'

Mussolini's militia had come calling.

The partisans grabbed their weapons and took up positions in the bedrooms. The women dragged ammunition boxes from the lower floors. Aldo had a machine gun and he began to fire; the others aimed pistols through window shutters. Enemy fire increased and lasted several minutes, and the defenders' response began to falter. They were running out of ammunition. Aldo looked through the window towards the barn and saw a glow. 'It's burning,' he said. 'There's nothing more we can do.'

His father, Alcide, replied, 'I'm not going to surrender to those dogs. We'll go down together. It's better to die than to live.'

Aldo stopped him and said: 'No, *Papa*, we have to consider the women and children. It's better to surrender.' The occupants of Campi Rossi crept down the stairs. They embraced each other.

The sons said to Genoveffa, 'Goodbye, *Mamma*. We will return soon, you will see. Stay calm.' She hugged them and stroked their hair.

'Better to die, better to die,' she murmured.

The doors were thrown open and the men walked into the yard with their hands above their heads. Alcide tried to run towards the cowshed, but a Fascist caught him. The farmer yelled, 'Cowards, at least let the animals go free.'

In one of the bedrooms, the sound of breaking glass had made Anatolij and John jump out of their beds. At first they were sleepy and did not understand what was going on, but they soon realised their predicament. The pair dressed quickly, hoping to escape, but they only had their Berettas; all the heavy weapons and ammunition had been packed the night before. To get to them, they had to reach the cellar.

The two partisans jumped into an enclosure where the horse was kept and calmed the startled animal. Anatolij banked up straw and a few rags and managed to clamber onto the portico through a small window. John followed and they climbed briskly onto the roof of the barn. The Cervis were firing from the windows.

All of a sudden the firing stopped, and once again the defenders heard the Blackshirts shout, 'Cervis, surrender!' There was another short burst of firing and then silence. Anatolij and John saw the Fascists throwing flaming torches. The hay in the barn began to burn violently while the shooting continued.

Someone called to Anatolij and John from the cowshed. The pair crept on all fours to the large window of the barn, as it sounded like Dante. 'We need the machine guns!' they shouted to him.

'We'll go and get them straight away, lads,' he replied. 'They're in the wine barrels in the cellar.'

The farmstead burnt like a giant bonfire, and dense white smoke covered the cowshed and the barn. The roof was about to collapse. John yelled, 'Jump down!' Anatolij fired two shots and threw himself on the portico and then onto a pile of fresh grass. John followed. They covered their faces with their hands and, firing the last shots, tried to get to the cellar through the opening in the fire. Anatolij recalled: 'We had almost reached it, when a terrible explosion threw me to the ground unconscious. I only revived when, as if in a dream, I heard someone say, "Ah, they're still alive!"'

When Anatolij opened his eyes he was staring into a leaden sky that was heavy with rain. He was handcuffed to John. On the wet road he saw his other companions with their hands tied—the seven Cervi brothers, Quarto Camurri, Dante, Johannes and Samuel. Blackshirts were everywhere.

A drunken Fascist with a bottle of wine in his hand stopped in front of Aldo and said to him, 'What shall we do with you now, *Bodigliano*? *Kaput*?'

'I am not a *Bodigliano*, but a Communist,' Aldo replied.

Seeing that the prisoners were about to be loaded onto a lorry, Alcide went towards the Fascist commander, Captain Cesare Pilati, and said to him in a resolute way, 'I want to go with my boys.' Turning towards Anatolij, Alcide saw his scant and singed clothing, took his own cloak off, and put it behind him. Then he climbed on the vehicle after them.

The women and children were left outside the burning farmstead. It was still raining heavily, and Alcide hoped that the rain would soon extinguish the flames; however, he later learned that the Fascists had looted the house and burned anything of value that they could not carry.

The news of the storming of the Cervi household quickly spread around the neighbourhood, and people came out onto the Via Emilia to see the captives pass by. The lorry drove into a patch of deep mud and had to be pulled out by two oxen. Here, the story diverges slightly; in his book *I miei sette figli* (*My Seven Sons*), written with journalist Renato Nicolai and published in 1955, Alcide said that the foreigners were offloaded onto another vehicle at a fork in the road. They were taken to prison in Parma, while he and the others went to the Servi gaol for political detainees in Reggio. However, in Anatolij's own account, *Sui Monti d'Italia* (*In the Mountains of Italy*), the Russian related that all the captives were sent to Servi, though the prisoners of war were transferred to Parma after a few days. However, he did confirm Alcide's next statement: 'Camurri remained with us, while Castellucci began to speak in French and said that he was a soldier of De Gaulle, and the Fascists believed him, and so put him together with the foreigners'.

The brothers were subjected to alternating bouts of interrogation and torture, but no one talked. Finally, an exasperated questioner told the captives that their lives would be saved if they joined the militia. 'We would not stoop so low,' one of the brothers replied for all of them. Shortly afterwards, they were moved to the second floor of the San Tommaso judicial gaol in Reggio. They spent Christmas there and persuaded the chief guard—named Pedrini—to smuggle a letter out to the farm. Dante had returned there after managing to escape from gaol in Parma. The family and the partisans worked on a plan of escape, though the attempt had to be deferred to New Year's Day while they sought police uniforms for five men to wear as disguises during the attempt.

On the evening of 27 December, the secretary of the commune of Bagnolo in Piano, Davide Onfiani, age forty-eight, was waiting on the platform of the railway station for a train to take him home to Correggio. A figure dressed in a peasant's cloak emerged from the fog and shot him dead at point-blank range; the unknown assailant then disappeared. The crime was immediately blamed on a group who had already become known as the 'Partisan Night

Executioners'. It was rumoured that they were British soldiers disguised as peasants (thanks to their cloaks) and using sophisticated weapons—small pistols equipped with silencers. An alternative suggestion was that they were Russians who had disembarked on the Romagna coast from Yugoslavia to prepare for the proletarian revolution in Emilia. In reality, however, the assassins were part of a small cell of Communists ordered to carry out sabotage on the plain and to target Fascist leaders.

The party chiefs met at Bagnolo later that evening and ordered a reprisal. A list of prisoners was inspected, and the names of the Cervis were underlined in red. At dawn the next day, the Fascists opened the door of the cell and ordered the brothers and Quarto Camurri out. Alcide was told to go back to sleep, as he was old. When he asked where his sons were going, he was told that it was to Parma for trial. The men were taken away quickly, with barely any time for farewells.

Instead of a court, the captives were taken before a firing squad on the range in Reggio. They were offered confession by a priest, but they said that they had no sins to repent; the Fascists were pleased by this because they were in a hurry. The commander asked which of the squad wanted the honour of firing. A soldier called Vulcano stepped forward, and others followed until there were enough for the execution to take place.

After the war, the Communist Party in Reggio was criticised for not having done enough to protect the Cervis or to save them once they were imprisoned. However, in 1979 Gismondo Veroni was keen to recall: 'The military committee was in continual contact with Aldo. I had this responsibility and met him for the last time on 23 November, two days before his arrest'. Veroni added that Aldo had enrolled as a party member in 1933 and maintained his membership until the end, as did several of his brothers. The differences that developed between him and the members of the Reggio party after 8 September were on the methods and timing of the partisan war, but they were never ideological. Aldo had a strong personality and an unusual fluency with language, but he could also be difficult and argumentative. Veroni concluded: 'We must recognise that more than us, he had a rage in his body. He was more exuberant and perhaps had even more courage'.[3]

Alcide was put in a cell with other political prisoners and knew nothing of the fate of his sons. At around 9 p.m. on 7 January 1944, the RAF attacked an aircraft and armaments factory and the adjoining airport near the prison; surrounding civilian areas were also hit. The prison began to shake, and the captives screamed at their gaolers to release them from the flames. The cell doors were hastily thrown open; a section of wall collapsed and the men flooded out. There was a follow-up raid by American aircraft during the following afternoon. In total, there were 264 civilian fatalities in Reggio.

Alcide made for the Via Emilia and the bridge over the Crostolo. As soon as he reached the railway line he called on some farming friends, and they lent him a bicycle. Alcide saw that his sons' caps were not on the hat stand at home; he awoke his wife and daughters-in-law and asked if they had any news of them. 'If you don't know anything, neither do we,' Genoveffa replied. Alcide tried to raise the women's morale by telling them that the brothers had been taken to the court in Parma for trial. They would cope well and return home sooner or later. If they had not gone to Parma, perhaps they had been deported to Poland to undertake forced labour.

On 21 January, a twenty-man detachment of Fascist militia carried out a raid on the rectory of the partisan priest Don Pasquino Borghi at Tapignola as the result of a denunciation. He was giving a sermon at Villa Minozzo at the time. The troops initially failed to find anything suspicious, and they were about leave when an opening at the end of a corridor attracted their attention. As they approached it, they were met by a hail of hand grenades thrown by partisans. The Fascists retreated, but that evening Don Pasquino was tracked down and arrested. He was shot on the firing range in Reggio nine days later, together with eight other partisans. The priest was posthumously awarded the Italian Gold Medal for Military Valour.

In the Cervi household, no one apart from Alcide seemed willing to talk about the fate of his children. After six weeks of silence, Genoveffa blurted out, 'Our sons will never return. All seven have been shot.' Alcide cried, his daughters-in-law consoled him.

Once the tears had stopped, he said, 'After a harvest comes another. We will go on.' With the help of his four daughters-in-law and (by then) eleven small grandchildren, Alcide cultivated the land and rebuilt the part of the farmhouse that had been destroyed by fire.

The Fascists returned to the Cervi farmstead at Gattatico on the evening of 10 October 1944, setting the hay loft on fire and running away. All the members of the family helped to throw water on the flames, but that night Genoveffa had a heart attack. She took to her bed and died on 14 December.

Dante Castellucci became a partisan leader under the pseudonym of Facio. He led the Guido Picelli detachment in the upper Parma Valley, and in March 1944 he won a notable victory over superior enemy forces at Lago Santo. However, when the group moved to the Pontremoli area they were accused of stealing airdrop supplies destined for another formation. Dante refused to answer the charges or to flee, and he was executed by a firing squad composed of partisans at dawn on 22 July; he was twenty-three. The questions around his death have never been fully resolved. Dante was posthumously awarded the Italian Silver Medal for Military Valour in 1963.

Anatolij escaped from gaol in Verona in the spring of 1944, returning to the Reggio area. He joined one of the action squads (SAP) operating on the plain and then crossed to the mountains of the neighbouring province of Modena, becoming the political commissar of a new Russian Battalion led by his countryman Vladimir Pereladov. Though mainly composed of Soviets, the formation also included several Italians, a squad of Czechoslovaks, a Yugoslav, two Britons and an Austrian. The brigade fought courageously in the campaign to liberate the mountain area, which led to the establishment of the free zone of Montefiorino on 18 June. After taking part in the unsuccessful defence of the 'partisan republic', the unit moved south and crossed enemy positions along the Gothic Line to the Fifth Army on 2 November. Anatolij helped repatriate his fellow Soviet soldiers at the end of the war, but he was arrested on his return to Russia due to the climate of suspicion towards soldiers captured by the Germans. He was released after three years and awarded his country's Order of the Patriotic War, First Class. Anatolij and Alcide met again in 1955, when the elderly Italian visited the Soviet Union.

Victor Pirogov (Danilo) also had an exemplary career as an Italian partisan after his encounters with the Cervis, adopting the new *nome di battaglia* of 'Modena'. In the summer of 1944, two detachments of Red Army troops united in a new Russian battalion under his command. The unit operated in the Enza Valley, in the province of Reggio, as part of the 144th *Garibaldi* Brigade until it joined the Allied Battalion, under Major Roy Farran, in March 1945—as we shall see in Chapter Sixteen.

Immediately after the war, the President of Italy pinned seven Silver Medals for Military Valour onto Alcide's chest—one each for Ettore, Ovidio, Agostino, Ferdinando, Aldo, Antenore and Gelindo. Alcide wrote in 1955:

> I looked after more than eighty prisoners in my house, mostly British and Americans ... Seven sons paid for this work of charity and their mother went with them due to a broken heart.[4]

The family farmhouse at Gattatico is now a museum dedicated to the Resistance and the history of the peasant movement.

6

Intelligence Gathering in Rome

Major d'Arcy Mander (from Youghal, in southern Ireland) was captured by Rommel's troops in the Western Desert on 1 June 1942, when serving as second in command of 4th Battalion of the Green Howards. The Germans overran the positions at Gazala after five days of hard fighting. The thirty-three-year-old regular soldier was flown to Italy. On 15 June he arrived at PG 75 Bari, and on 8 July was transferred to PG 29 Veano—located in a hamlet of the Commune of Vigolzone, in the province of Piacenza.

The camp was housed in the Villa Alberoni, a former stately home that was being used as a seminary for training priests. PG 29 had opened on 1 May 1942 as a prison for Allied officers of field rank. There were frequent escape attempts, although men only managed to leave the immediate vicinity of the camp on a few occasions, and all were ultimately recaptured.

The villa is accessed along the gentle slope of a 2.5-mile-long avenue of limes and mulberry trees, and is surrounded by a large garden planted with evergreens. There is a panoramic view over the Nure Valley and down across the plain.

On the eve of the Armistice in 1943 there were 268 prisoners, of whom 206 were officers. Sixty-two 'other ranks' were their 'batmen'—valets or attendants. Two hundred and fifty-four of the men were British. The other fourteen were Australian, Canadian, Irish, Maltese, New Zealander, Polish and South African. The senior British officer was Colonel George Younghusband, and the Italian commandant was Colonel Cornaggia Medici Castiglioni. The Italian garrison numbered 150, comprising soldiers and *Carabinieri*—the army corps that is also a police force.

Rumours of the Armistice arrived at Veano on 8 September, a few hours before the official announcement via the girlfriend of one of the Italian sergeants, who was a telephone operator in Piacenza. Colonel Medici Castiglioni asked to speak urgently with Colonel Younghusband and give him the news. Shortly afterwards, the camp staff and the prisoners mingled in the courtyard to listen to the radio announcement over loudspeakers; the ending of hostilities was greeted with ringing cheers. However, the SBO addressed the prisoners in the dining hall and ordered them to remain in the camp; no one knew what the Germans were doing, and several thousand prisoners loose in northern Italy would add to the confusion significantly. The men were told to pack and to be ready to leave at a moment's notice. An alarm signal and a bugle summons were laid down and reserve rations issued.

The commandant and garrison joined Catholic prisoners at a mass of thanks in the morning. The Italian colonel was perplexed because he had received no orders; after consulting his officers, he decided to set the captives free. An 80-foot section of the wire fence was cut, and the men rushed into the surrounding fields and houses. News arrived that Germans were fighting Italians in Piacenza, and in the afternoon defeated Italian troops began to arrive at the camp. Over two-thirds of the guards deserted during the night.

On the morning of 10 September, Colonel Younghusband announced that Colonel Medici Castiglioni had told him that he no longer had enough soldiers to guarantee the safety of the prisoners in the event of a German attack. The SBO informed his men that they were now free to make their own choices, although he would remain there and recommended that others did so too.

The Italian Commandant obtained supplies of currency, and each prisoner was given a few hundred lire. An early lunch was served. Just after midday, groups of the prisoners began to march into the hills behind the camp, while a few individuals changed into civilian clothing and took the electric train that, in those days, ran up the valley from Piacenza to Bettola. The enemy was only about 4 miles away. A few minutes later the alarm was sounded; the Germans fired random shots into the surrounding woods, looted the buildings, and failed to capture a single prisoner. The official record from the British War Office simply noted: 'Information was received the Germans were approaching … and the whole camp scattered into the countryside'.

The escapers faced four main choices. They could remain in the area until circumstances became clearer, move north towards Switzerland, move south towards friendly forces, or move west, to the coast, where Allied landings were rumoured. An escape line to Switzerland was created by Lieutenant-Colonel Norman Boddington of the Royal Engineers. He was helped by a fellow sapper, Major Tony Dobson. The local arrangements were handled by a garage-owner who hired cars to the Germans. His activities were eventually discovered, and he was subsequently shot. The escape line evacuated many servicemen, including Colonel Boddington and Major Dobson, but at the end of November it succumbed to Fascist attack. Eight prisoners were recaptured and deported to camps in Greater Germany.

D'Arcy Mander noted that more than twice as many Allied escapers and evaders crossed Allied lines in Italy as the Swiss border during the war:

> It is perhaps a tribute to the Italian people that, although Switzerland was so close as to be visible, yet a very large proportion of the prisoners when their chance came at the Armistice chose not the short comparatively easy trip to Switzerland but the route south to the Eighth Army, which was a very long way indeed by comparison.[1]

D'Arcy left Veano on 10 September, accompanied by Trooper Joseph Maddox, who was one of the batmen, and Majors Bill Syme, Royal Artillery, and James Marshall, Seaforth Highlanders. D'Arcy had an aunt in Florence—Eileen Coutts, the widow of his uncle Reginald. As she was the only person in Italy that any of them had ever heard of except for the Pope and Mussolini, they decided to make their way along the Apennines and try and get in touch with her.

Roads were crossed with great care, and a wide berth was given to villages and towns. Every evening the escapers would find a suitably isolated farmhouse and ask for food and shelter. They found that the poorest people would willingly share what little they had, while the rich had more to lose and were not so welcoming. In October the escapers reluctantly decided that four was too large a party, splitting into pairs; Bill and James succeeded in making the long journey to the Gran Sasso range in the Abruzzo, but they were then killed by an avalanche.

D'Arcy and Joseph reached the hills around Fiesole at the end of October. They found hundreds of escaped prisoners of war living on local farms. Together with Father Bonomi (the local priest) and Corporal H. D. Medway, Coldstream Guards, d'Arcy helped arrange guides and transport to get the men moving south. He later did the same with fugitive servicemen on Monte Morello, near Florence.

D'Arcy made contact with his aunt and she brought them money and cigarettes in the hills. They met later at the Villa Diana in Fiesole. Arrangements were made for an escape, as he related in his report to MI9, given in England in August 1944:

> On 7 November I left Acone in a motor ambulance which I had obtained from an organisation in Florence. I had with me about seven ex-prisoners of war and intended heading for the British lines. We went to Rufina and Pontassieve. On the road to Arezzo we were ambushed by Germans and Italians. I think we must have been given away.[2]

The Germans drove the prisoners to the Rovezzano barracks on the eastern outskirts of Florence. The next day they were taken to the railway station and put in a third-class carriage alongside other escapers and Italian deserters. The train moved once it was dark. As they were leaving Sesto at around midnight, d'Arcy got through a window, climbed along the footboard, and sat on a buffer. He was joined by two members of a parachute battalion—Lieutenant Playford and Private Hull. As the lights of Prato came into view, the train slowed, and all three jumped successfully. Joseph stayed on board and remained in captivity for the rest of the war.

D'Arcy returned to the Monte Morello district with Lieutenant Playford, and Private Hull joined them three days later. The Major learned that on 12 November his aunt and most of the other people in the villa at Fiesole had been arrested, and that their property had been seized. They were tried and sentenced to death, although these sentences were later commuted to long terms of imprisonment. However, they were released when most of Tuscany was liberated in the summer of 1944.

D'Arcy left the area on 26 November, accompanied by South African lieutenants Jack Selikman and Sandy Stewart from PG 47 Modena. They intended to cross the British lines, but if that proved impossible they would go to Rome and see what could be done from there. On the way south they met two other prisoners who had escaped from a German prison train. Captain Donald Macaulay was a doctor at PG 49 Fontanellato. Captain Marcus Kane Burman was the dentist. He recognised his fellow South Africans as patients from his practice back home. The two groups met four times on the way to Rome. Marcus and Donald put d'Arcy's group in touch with a member of the Resistance at Soriano, who provided shelter and sent them with two guides to Vignanello to catch the train for Rome. The escapers were told that they would be handed over to the 'Organisation'. The party arrived in the enemy capital on the evening of 9 December. The guides returned to the country within forty-eight hours.

Following the German occupation, Pope Pius XII had ordered that convents and monasteries in Rome, extraterritorial property of the Vatican, should be opened to anti-Fascists and Jews. Monsignor Hugh O'Flaherty and other Catholics broadened the humanitarian effort to include escaped prisoners of war. The priest was a citizen of the neutral Irish Free State and Notary of the Holy Office; he had served as a diplomat and as the secretary and interpreter to the Papal Nuncio to the camps in Italy until dismissed under German pressure in December 1942.

The secret welfare organisation was mainly financed by the British Minister to the Holy See, Sir D'Arcy Osborne. So as not to compromise his diplomatic status, he entrusted day to day arrangements to his butler, John May. Funds were also provided by the American Chargé d'Affaires, Harold Tittmann, and by Prince Filippo Andrea Doria Pamphilj, who was in hiding in the Trastevere district. By the time of the liberation, the Rome Organisation had the names of 3,925 escapers and evaders on its books, of whom 1,695 were British, 896 South African, 429 Russian, 425 Greek, 185 American and 295 from another twenty countries.

In November 1943 the British minister had appointed Major Sam Derry, another escaper from a German prison train, as military head of the body, which became known as the British Organisation in Rome for Assisting Allied Escaped Prisoners of War. Its aim was to keep the growing number of escapers converging on the Rome area out of enemy hands by finding places for the men to live and ensuring that they regularly received food, clothing and medical supplies. As well as clerics, diplomats and aristocrats, the service relied upon an army of ordinary Italian men and women who ignored daily broadcasts on Rome Radio that promised death to anyone providing aid and comfort to the enemy.

The newcomers' first night in Rome was spent in an empty flat. In the morning, d'Arcy decided to visit Captain Leonardo Trippi, Military Attaché at the Swiss Legation, whom he remembered from an inspection visit to Veano. The Major was surprised to meet another Briton in the waiting room, evader Lieutenant Robert 'Tug' Wilson. He had teamed up with Captain 'Pip' Gardner VC from Camp 49 at Fontanellato. D'Arcy poured out his story and Wilson said that he knew just the right man to find him accommodation. In the Vatican he introduced the Major to Branko Bitler, who was described by another escaper as a short, thick-set, wild-eyed, twenty-eight-year-old Croatian theatre director. He had had come to Rome to carry the fight to the enemy. He was a member of one of the most active partisan groups in Rome— the *Movimento Comunista d'Italia,* known popularly as the '*Bandiera Rossa*' after the underground newspaper it published. Branko was working with one of the leaders, who was called Italo Nebulanti. Part of their activities involved helping Allied escapers, and they were in frequent contact with Major Sam Derry and the secret rescue organisation in the Vatican.

Branko took d'Arcy, Jack and Sandy through leafy side streets to the Via Domenico Chelini in the northern Parioli district. They entered a large block of flats via the garage entrance. Inside a spacious apartment, the three escapers found eight or nine other prisoners of war. Priests from the Vatican brought food for the men every day. An attractive, blonde Jewess from Austria called Herta Katerina Habernig lived in the basement flat and did their cooking, washing and mending.

The number of prisoners in the building increased steadily. One day, Captains Macaulay and Kane Burman, their two friends from Fontanellato, arrived. D'Arcy was concerned about the security of the organisation and urged Branko to find a smaller place for them. In the meantime, the Major took a leading part in ensuring windows were shuttered, in keeping the inmates out of sight, and in introducing bell signals and alarm drills.

D'Arcy went out every day to meet people and to try to find friends who would provide shelter in case anything went wrong. He especially remembered the first people Branko introduced him to. Laszlo and Nora Kiss had a flat in Piazza Fiume; he was a debonair Hungarian actor turned filmmaker, and she was a petite Russian émigré who taught dance. Another contact, Daniele, was a young Italian who had been captured on the Russian front. He convinced the Soviets that he was a good Communist, was given his freedom, and married a Russian girl. The Major recalled that the couple had returned to Italy in mysterious circumstances:

> I suspect that he pretended to be a Communist in Russia, but I don't think he was ever a committed one and he certainly was not one of the Stalin worshipping Italian crowd. Neither was he a Fascist like his father, and it became quite obvious that he wasn't on our side either. I came to the conclusion that he worked for himself and nobody else.[3]

On 7 January 1944, Branko announced that he had found a flat for d'Arcy, Jack and Sandy. They were to move out the next day. Branko brought the porter of the new block along to begin clearing their possessions. D'Arcy was appalled at the breach of security when he found the stranger in the same room as the prisoners, but he concentrated on making arrangements for the departure.

The following morning, uniformed SS men raided the flat that Nebulanti and Branko had found for 'Tug' Wilson and 'Pip' Gardner. The escapers and the Communist leader were seized and taken to the Regina Coeli gaol. Two Gestapo agents were left with a cook, who by mischance was aware of the existence of the other flats; he also knew the secret signal on the doorbells (three short and one long) necessary to gain admission. The man was subjected to rough interrogation and revealed everything.

The agents accompanied the cook to the Via Domenico Chelini flat. One of Major Derry's lieutenants, John Furman, answered the door. The men told him that the flat had been raided and that Wilson and Gardner had been arrested. They entered the dining room, and John said, 'I can't understand why the cook brought you along with him. It was nice of you to keep him company, but it seems so unnecessary. Before you go, would you mind showing me your identity cards?'

There was a roar of German voices in the corridor outside, and instead of identity cards the two men pulled out revolvers. Half a dozen heavily armed SS men poured in, and the prisoners of war and Branko and Herta were lined up against a wall with their hands above their heads. The cook also led the Germans to another flat in Via Firenze, near the Opera House, where three South Africans were rounded up.

Meanwhile, d'Arcy was in the city looking for supplies for the new flat. When he returned to Via Domenico Chelini at about 3.30 p.m., he gave the signal on the bell and the door opened. The major recalled:

> Nobody was visible because nobody was there except for two figures in uniform, one of whom held a rifle pointed at my stomach and the other who said in German, 'What do you want?'

The soldiers bundled d'Arcy into a front room as they awaited further callers, but did not bother to check a shuttered window. He was able to jump through it to the street below. Cesare Coen, the fiancé of Herta, was on the pavement and accompanied the Major to the apartment of Laszlo and Nora Kiss. She immediately rang Daniele and had a rapid conversation with him in Russian. About fifteen minutes later, a car drove up and Daniele entered the flat in the full splendour of an SS uniform. D'Arcy gasped, but Nora put her hand on his arm and said that she would explain later. She talked to Daniele again; he looked pale and alarmed, and a few minutes later he drove off with Cesare.

D'Arcy learned that the Via Domenico Chelini flat was owned by people who had been arrested by the SS's Security Service, the *Sicherheitsdienst* (SD). Daniele was one of their Italian employees and had taken part in that raid. However, he was a double agent, and since the flat was empty and unused, he had thought it would make a good safehouse for prisoners of war. Soon after returning to Rome from Russia he had been involved in a street fracas and arrested, but was bailed out by his father, a colonel in the Italian Army, through whose good offices he was offered a post with the German SS. Daniele had consulted Nora before accepting. After thinking it over carefully, she told him to go ahead—provided he kept them informed on what was going on.

Nora told Daniele that when the news broke of the raid at the SS HQ, he was to appear astonished and furious. He was to state that he had arranged for the prisoners to be in his flat as a lure for a very important Russian general who was expected to be in Rome shortly; the trap had been sprung just when it had been set.

Daniele's cover was preserved and he and his wife went to live in the flat, ostensibly to catch the very important Russian general. D'Arcy even stayed there sometimes because he reckoned that a twice-raided flat occupied by an SS man would be just about the safest spot in Rome. The Major reflected:

> I realised the importance of having Daniele in the SS and ... perhaps I owed my safety in Rome more than a little to him. I didn't need to do anything much about him because he and Nora already had excellent working arrangements.

She would often get warnings of a raid, an impending arrest, a house which was being watched, or a tapped telephone line. Nora would go and warn the people concerned—although if they were Communists, the advice might be ignored.

The captured prisoners of war from the transit flats were soon deported to Germany. When d'Arcy went to see Major Derry and Monsignor O'Flaherty in the Vatican, he found that they already knew all about the raid. Branko had been separated from the others; he was interrogated and tortured in the Via Tasso SS dungeon. On 28 January he was tried by the German Tribunal of War at the Hotel Flora, together with ten other members of the *Bandiera Rossa*. They were sentenced to death and executed at Forte Bravetta on 2 February. Monsignor O'Flaherty recalled that he had received a note that Branko had somehow smuggled out in the morning. O'Flaherty recalled, 'He wanted me to know that he never opened his mouth once.'

Herta was sentenced to five years' imprisonment, which she served in her native Austria. At the end of the war she returned to settle in Rome. D'Arcy blamed the porter of the new flat for the SS raids, while most protagonists have pointed the finger at the cook from the premises of 'Tug' Wilson and 'Pip' Gardner.

Through Italian friends who periodically went into the countryside to obtain food and other goods to sell on the black market, d'Arcy received messages from prisoners of war requesting money, medical assistance, clothing, boots, or just news. He went to see Monsignor O'Flaherty at the German College, who gave him money for the fugitives and also arranged for help to be provided by local priests. However, the Major recalled, 'I tried to manage my own affairs without involving him in any way in my various undercover activities.'

By the time the flat was raided, d'Arcy had already found a number of trustworthy families who were willing to provide shelter. It was to these contacts that he now turned. There was another reason that he was keen to circulate, as he recalled:

I could speak German, I had studied the German Army and could recognize the badges worn by German officers and soldiers and could therefore identify units and be in a position to send information to the Allies. As I got around I met people who supplied me with all kinds of information. I knew a chap who gave the details of all the rail traffic passing through Rome. I met Italian officers on the run and I had one living on nearly every main road in and out of Rome and they kept watch for and reported all military convoys. And, of course, there was Daniele ensconced in the German security headquarters. I didn't want to hide and be walled up as some PoWs were. I wanted to be active and do something to help, and I was able to send a lot of varied information to the Allies, and also help other less fortunate prisoners living in the mountains outside Rome.[4]

It was easy for d'Arcy to move around and to get to know so many people in such a short time. He used to go to lawyers acting for wealthy clients who were doing very well out of Mussolini's government contracts, and he would borrow money from them in exchange for an IOU. This would be produced later as evidence that the client had been supporting the Allies all the time. D'Arcy used false documents in the name of 'Pietro Bartoli'. He worked with a variety of Italian dissidents and black marketeers, Communists, Jews, Yugoslavs and émigrés. John May, the British minister's butler, also cashed a large cheque for him, drawn on Messrs. Holts Bankers, using the rate of exchange set by the Allies in the south of 400 lire to the pound.

One day, the Major was lying on the grass in a quiet part of the Villa Borghese Park, waiting for a German helper called Anneliese, who was married to an Italian captain missing in the Balkans. Shortly after she arrived, the park filled up with *Carabinieri* looking for deserters of military age. D'Arcy stood up when they asked for his papers. He showed them his identity card, which said that he was a sculptor by profession and listed his address as a bombed-out house in Rome. His questioner was a Neapolitan and the Major addressed him in his best German. He showed him a certificate that said he was a mobilised member of the War Wounded Rehabilitation Organisation. D'Arcy's receding hair made him look older than he was, so they believed him and he was able to saunter away with Anneliese.

The Major's information-gatherers were mainly Italian Army officers on the run. He was in touch with the 8th Army through the use of underground wireless operators; he knew that the messages were getting through because he received replies. However, the organisation was makeshift and tenuous. All this changed with the arrival of a former Italian artillery captain using the cover name 'Pietro'. He had been sent through the German lines to set up a network of mobile wireless operators to transmit intelligence to the Allies. The agent contacted d'Arcy and (after they had checked one another's credentials through the British authorities) they made arrangements to communicate via the Italian's girlfriend, Rosina. She met the Major in a variety of locations, and regularly passed on instructions, warnings and news of events in Rome.

One day it was Pietro himself who came to the rendezvous. He reported that information was required about the organisation the Germans were planning to leave behind in Rome when they were finally driven out. D'Arcy was ordered to take an interest. He told Pietro to reply: 'With great pleasure. The matter is already in hand.' Pietro gave the Major a stern lecture on the danger he would bring everybody else if he got caught, but it was the Italian who was eventually captured and shot.

D'Arcy and Laszlo Kiss used to meet for a drink in various bars, coffee houses and hotels in Rome. One of their favourite haunts was the Hotel Eden, which was also popular with the German Army. One Saturday, Laszlo visited the hotel with his wife, Nora. They were surprised to be refused admission but were finally let in by a porter who knew them from their trips to see a Polish lady resident. While Nora went upstairs to visit her friend, Laszlo sauntered into the lounge, which was full of German officers. He listened to them discussing the plan of attack to be mounted on the Anzio bridgehead on Monday morning. The pair quickly found the Major. He was not due to meet Rosina until Monday, but he located Pietro via another of the operator's informants. The captain got the message through in good time; it was acted on, and the attack was beaten off.

At the end of May the weather got very hot and sultry, and there were signs that the hunt for d'Arcy was also warming up. There had been several losses in his group—particularly among the wireless operators—and he was becoming too well-known for his safety and that of his friends. It was becoming too dangerous to go to the Vatican, and there had been plenty of warnings to get out of Rome, but he had no wish to return to the life of a fugitive in the countryside.

Laszlo and Nora's flat was raided by the Security Police, but they did not find anything suspicious apart from the telephone number of a well-known black marketeer. Later, Laszlo was arrested by the Italian police for trying to sell gold on the black market. D'Arcy recalled: 'We told Daniele to go and tell them that the Germans wanted him and to get him out, which he did to the fury of the Italians. He also got the gold, but he only handed Laszlo over to us.'

In the last days of occupation, the Major bumped into Captain Denti, who had been Italian interpreter at the prison camp of Veano and had called his name in numerous roll calls. Fortunately, the officer didn't seem to recognise him, and the Major passed quietly by.

At the beginning of June, D'Arcy went to ground in a friend's flat for one or two days. On the fourth, he recalled, Rome was at last, miraculously, still: 'There was no battle, no shot or shell fire … it was obvious that something was in the air.' Despite the evening curfew, the Major slipped out of the flat and walked towards the Piazza del Popolo, which was lit by the full moon. He went across the deserted square to the far side and saw the shape of a tank and some figures in the shadows; it was the advance guard of an American ranger battalion of the Fifth Army.

D'Arcy hoped to get home as soon as possible. Most of his work was done, but he had been asked to stay to deal with the German agents. He was given a uniform, money and a car to get around the city. D'Arcy recalled that he and Nora turned to Daniele for information on the organisation the Germans had left behind, but that he appeared somewhat slow in providing the information they wanted:

> I am afraid that Daniele was playing the double game for all he was worth, and up to the very last. I had to get him out of gaol twice as the Communists

had him arrested as an SS man and one can quite understand that he wanted perhaps not just money, but at least security, in exchange for his information.[5]

Many of the Italians who had been recruited as German agents surrendered their wireless sets, codes and money. Daniele finally talked and the entire network fell into Allied hands. D'Arcy did not know what happened to him after he left Rome, but he was aware that he was considering going to South America. He speculated that Daniele might have been able to continue his little game of being all things to all men and true to no one but himself.

In fact, Daniele's fate was entirely different. His real name was Ubaldo Cipolla, and he was soon re-arrested. It was said that he had infiltrated the *Bandiera Rossa* partisan group with another German collaborator called Biagio Roddi, and he had worked with the head of its press and propaganda section, Ezio Malatesta. Cipolla had taken part in the roundup of the formation's leaders after anti-Fascist leaflets had been scattered in cinemas on 6 December 1943. He lured Malatesta and other partisans to a rendezvous on the pretext of organising their departure from Rome, and pointed out those to be arrested to the SS. They were among the eleven partisans executed at Forte Bravetta on 2 February 1944. As we have seen, they included Branko Bitler—d'Arcy's first helper in Rome.

The charges against Cipolla were found to be true, and on 31 May 1947 he was sentenced to life imprisonment by the Special Assizes Court of Rome. However, over the following nine years there were three references to the Appeal Court and interventions by the Supreme Court; as a result, the term of the sentence was steadily reduced. Ubaldo Cipolla was released from prison on 26 December 1953.

Before leaving Rome, D'Arcy broadcast a prearranged message on Italian radio: '*Meriela sta bene*.' ('Meriel is well.') She was the daughter he had not yet seen, whose photograph was shown to all their hosts until it was lost when he was arrested near Florence. The Major explained:

> I wanted to thank those brave people who had sheltered us and fed us on our journey. I wanted to tell them that their efforts had been successful in my case and in many other cases, and encourage them to go on assisting prisoners still at large in the north.[6]

D'Arcy left Rome on 1 July 1944 and returned to the United Kingdom via Algiers and Rabat. He was decorated with the Distinguished Service Order (DSO) for his undercover operations in the city. The citation reads:

> This officer was taken prisoner in Africa and transferred to Italy, but succeeded in escaping from the train, in which he was being moved to another camp, and eventually arrived in Rome in December 1943.

Here he got in touch with a pro-Allied Italian intelligence organisation, which was transmitting military intelligence by wireless to the Allies in southern Italy.

Major Mander himself obtained a considerable amount of valuable information, including the date on which the main German counter-attack would be launched against the Anzio bridgehead.

He also did useful work for a period of six months in the counter-intelligence field, in the course of which he showed great ability, resource and courage, the result of which was the virtual elimination of enemy agents within a short time after the capture of Rome.

Major Mander was twice arrested by the Gestapo and only succeeded in freeing himself by the greatest ingenuity.

On his return to England, d'Arcy was posted to the Staff College and then the Control Commission in Germany. He served in the army for another eighteen years, leaving with the rank of Colonel in 1963. D'Arcy joined the firm of Sir Owen Williams and Partners, consulting engineers, and worked for them for over twenty years, retiring at the age of seventy-five.

7

Partisan Warfare in Tuscany

On the morning of 3 January 1944 a force of fifty Fascist militia and *Carabinieri* surrounded a group of partisans in a stone barn in the mountains north-west of Florence. The rebels were twelve Italians, two Russians, two Yugoslavs and a British officer, Captain Stuart Clink Hood of the Highland Light Infantry. Born in Scotland, he was secretly a former member of the British Communist Party when he joined the army in 1940 at the age of twenty-five.

Stuart was one of more than 500 officers and men held at PG 49 Fontanellato in the summer of 1943:

> Early one morning in July 1943, I saw a young soldier go into the office of the commandant, take the portrait of Mussolini, which was inevitably placed above the desk, throw it on the floor and jump on it. I knew that something important had happened. In fact, Mussolini had been deposed. The pages of the newspapers began to appear with white columns in which the news had been censured, but they spoke of events such as a Communist meeting presided over by Giovanni Roveda and of political activity by the Socialists and others. This was a strange period under the rule of Marshal Badoglio and a moment of standstill among the ranks of the Italian governing class and the armed forces. The Allies had landed in Sicily. We sat down and waited, noting the growing number of German troops.
>
> Then on 9 September we were called on parade by our bugler. We were told that the Italian commandant was sorry, but he did not have enough weapons to give us to fight the Germans, which he wanted to resist, and that he would release us from the barbed wire. So we found ourselves in the middle of the Emilian fields, not knowing where to go or what to do.

Together with Captain Edward 'Ted' Mumford of the Third Gurkha Rifles, Stuart found shelter on a local farm called 'Toccalmatto'—'The Madman's Lot'. Ironically, the family's name was *Tedeschi*, meaning 'The Germans'.

After a few days, the pair decided that Allied landings in the north were unlikely and decided to make their way towards friendly forces in the south. Stuart recalled that they were two men in their late twenties with nothing in common except the shock of capture and the boredom of captivity:

> Ted, broad and powerful, brown, with an Asian look and a thin black moustache, as if he had been assimilated to his own squat soldiers … Myself, tall, thin, asthenic, with a narrow head like a collie-dog's.

Their route lay across the Emilian Apennines to Tuscany. The son of the farmhouse guided them as far as the railway line. Ted left behind a gold ring, saying that he would return for it 'after the war'. The pair relied for food and shelter on the subsistence farmers and repaid their hospitality by working in the fields. The escapers learned about the chestnut and wine harvests and how to plough and use a hoe.

Stuart related that the peasant houses catered for all of life's essentials—warmth, food and a place to sleep—and that the residents were friendly:

> We found that their enemy was authority—the landlord and his factor, the state and its inspectors, the *Duce* and the Pope. For them Fascism meant authority. Fascism took their wheat for the communal grain pool, their copper pots for the driving bands of shells, their sons for the wars. It gave them nothing in return. Its enemies, in simple logic, must be their friends.[1]

Two weeks after leaving Fontanellato, the two escapers were still on the wrong side of the Apennines. They felt even more cut off than in the camp, but they decided that the Allies would soon advance before the winter set in. If not, they would try to find the partisans. Stuart recalled: 'Perhaps we stayed so long in this crude Arcadia because we were still not ready to face the world. Yet we had strong reasons for action.'

On 10 November, in deep snow, Stuart and Ted crossed the Abetone Pass (1,388 metres) into Tuscany, finding shelter at Pian della Fava, near the village of Antelminelli, in the province of Lucca—about 44 miles north-west of Florence. By the beginning of December, the pair had reached the hills above Pistoia. Stuart related that by chance they met a partisan liaison officer called Franco and faced a dilemma:

> Up to now we had been unarmed fugitives, subject always to treachery and recapture, liable, in the worst of cases, to be obscurely shot. But our luck had held … Now we had to decide whether to accept the hazards of the *franc-tireur* [sniper]. We had a couple of weeks to make up our minds.[2]

Shortly before Christmas, the pair joined a partisan group. In a speech given at Portsmouth University in 2000—entitled 'Partisan Memories'—Stuart recalled:

> We were no longer alone, but were being drawn into a web whose centre lay in Florence with the Committee of National Liberation. I did so because I had become a soldier in order to fight in what I considered an anti-Fascist war. It was as a fellow anti-Fascist that the group welcomed me. Finding my name difficult, they dubbed me Carlino.

The group had been formed by Sergeant Major Lanciotto Ballerini. He was a tall, fair-haired man in his thirties—square-faced, handsome, and with the broken nose of a professional boxer. His family had a butcher's shop in the little town of Campi Bisenzio. Stuart related: 'He was a fighter, a Communist, innocent of doctrine, fearless himself, but with no knack of leading men.' On the Armistice, Lanciotto was on garrison duty in Florence owing to a leg wound sustained during the Abyssinian campaign. He loaded arms and ammunition onto a truck and hid them on the slopes of Monte Morello. He was gradually joined by a mixture of Italians and escaped prisoners of war who wanted to take part in the armed struggle.

By December 1943 the group numbered seventeen. Once Christmas passed, Lanciotto announced that they were to move off to the high mountains in two stages. The main formation was to cross to the bare ridge of Calvana, which runs down towards the plain around Prato. Meanwhile, the political commissar (known as 'Toto') would lead a detachment to find a cache of mortar bombs on Monte Morello. They were to remove the explosive and send it down to the liberation committee in Florence. Ted left with the group, and they climbed to an upland farmhouse where they spent the night. In the morning, the men unearthed the mortar bombs. Ted managed to remove the small explosive charges, and soon he had a haversack full of them. The next day, while the group were waiting to move off to re-join the main formation, a boy arrived with the news that they had been ambushed.

Stuart related that he and Ted never met again in Italy:

> Chance took him to Florence to wait for a guide across the Swiss frontier. Boredom made him chafe at the waiting. Taking a train to Venice, he looked in vain for a fishing boat to carry him down the Adriatic, put up in a hotel full of German officers, and returned safely to Florence. From Swiss internment he passed back to his battalion on the Italian front. The end of the campaign brought him back to the farm of Toccalmatto and the Tedeschi family. Reaching up to a hiding place in the wall, behind a fly-spotted photograph, they gave him back his ring.[3]

Stuart recalled that the motive that had led him to the Calvana was the rebellion against the social norms that had surrounded him as an adolescent:

> My father, a young worker who had taken his degree after years of hard labour, was the headmaster of a small school in a little town in Scotland, which we left later to move to a fishing community in the east, where I was brought up. In social terms, I was born into the lower middle class and imbibed the ethics of Protestantism and the Scottish tradition of egalitarianism … We enjoyed a secure position, even though we were far from being considered well off. It was inevitable that I would have to study and follow in my father's footsteps and become a teacher. We did not talk about politics much at home. It was something that went on in the world that was suited to other people and not to us.

The main partisan group reached a cluster of peasant houses called Valibona in the commune of Calenzano. They took shelter in a long, stone barn on the slope above the hamlet. The men were armed with an assortment of rifles, a supply of small Italian hand grenades and a Breda light machine gun. The weather was bitterly cold with snow and a bitter frost.

On the morning of 3 January, Stuart was woken by one of the Russians—a sergeant major—with the whispered word 'Fascists!' The pair crawled about in the straw and shook the sleepers awake, muffling their protests with a hand over their mouths. Lanciotto and Stuart crept along the top of the straw to the upper floor and the machine gun. The operator—Luigi Ventroni, a broad-shouldered Sardinian who was also their cook—was lying beside it, with the butt pressed into his shoulder and his finger on the trigger. Lanciotto crawled out before Stuart onto the threshing floor, and they knelt under the cover of its low wall.

The partisans could hear the tramping of feet. Suddenly, a detachment of militia, marching in threes, came out of the hollows of the hills. Lanciotto gave Stuart a signal to cover him and threw a hand grenade. When the explosion came, the machine gun began to fire from inside the barn. Two short bursts went out, but then it jammed. The militia had broken ranks in a confusion of shouts and yells, and Lanciotto stood up and harried them with grenades; he and Stuart then tried to get back into the barn. However, a burst of fire forced them out on to the threshing floor again. The machine gun jammed once more and the Sardinian tore off the magazine, swearing terribly. Lanciotto and Stuart threw themselves past him and fell face-down in the straw.

Stuart related that the smell of cordite was heavy inside the barn:

> The lower floor was clear. In the quiet of the first cold light I was seized with a wave of terror, like a child in the night stumbling on the thought of death. I looked at my watch. It was six o'clock. In a couple of hours, I thought, I

shall be dead, and sat with my carbine on my knees, automatically stuffing my pockets with rounds. I had a terrible wish not to be there, to be spirited away, to float up to the ceiling.[4]

The Sardinian was on his side in the doorway, wrestling with the machine gun. Stuart crept over to him and looked out beyond the threshing floor to a long slope of grass peppered with patches of snow and grey stones; now and again, a stone seemed to move. Far down the incline, an officer wearing a greatcoat and a helmet was walking around and gesticulating. Stuart aimed and fired at him with his carbine, but he did not see the strike of the bullet.

From time to time the machine-gunner would fire a burst and then stop, and then back would come the enemy response. The Fascists had the door covered, but most of their fire was caught by the low threshing floor. Stuart felt a sharp blow on his arm and saw that his weapon was covered in blood; however, it was only a scratch between his finger and thumb.

Lanciotto and the Russians were firing from the lower doorway. There was a slow movement uphill, and the firing became continuous. Stuart was dazed with noise. Lanciotto announced that they could break out at their discretion, and Stuart told the Sardinian, but he said nothing and struggled to clear another stoppage. Stuart went down to the lower door to find that Lanciotto was gone. The Russians were there with couple of boys; one by one they ran, crouching, into the open, jumping into a ditch by the side of the wall.

Stuart recalled: 'Above the barn, the hillside was suddenly naked and open. I ran fast with someone at my side, making for the cover of an outcrop of rock.' The militia were climbing up from stone to stone. Stuart fired at them. The soil beside him was flicked up by a series of spurts from answering machine-gun fire. The militia officer was standing in the open; Stuart aimed and fired until the bolt of his carbine jammed. Someone was crawling along next to him; it was Mirko, a young Yugoslav student, who began to run, hard, towards the crest 300 yards away. Stuart threw down his gun and followed.

The battle lasted for at least two hours. When it was over, the barn was on fire, the partisan leader, Lanciotto Ballerini, was dead, and so were two of his men. Eight more were captured, of whom four had been wounded; only Stuart and three other rebels escaped. The peasant families from the nearby houses were taken away as prisoners.

Stuart was picked up by the Resistance and hidden in a peasant house for several weeks. He learned here that Lanciotto had died and that casualties on the enemy side included an important militia commander from Prato and a boy of fifteen.

Stuart told the Portsmouth Conference:

The outcome, it was clear to me, had been determined by the failure to post sentries. I had tried to persuade the group to do so, but had failed. Should

I, I wondered, have insisted? But my situation had been difficult. My rank as an officer in the British army had no validity in these circumstances. Besides, I could not be seen to undermine the authority of their commander. A contributory factor to the failure of the defence had been that the machine gun repeatedly jammed. A couple of days before, the machine gunner had replaced every fifth round in the ammunition belt with a round of tracer. I suspected that this, for some reason, had caused the trouble. I subsequently learned that he was burned to death in the barn.

By the beginning of March 1944, Stuart had made his way almost as far south as Siena. He was recruited by a group of partisans known as the *Raggruppamento Monte Amiata* and spent four months with them. The main personalities were Italian officers, and their leader was Major Terosi—a diminutive and ginger-haired man whose mother was from Yorkshire. Stuart assumed that they were monarchists, but he in 1999 he learned that the formation had been founded in Siena by the republican Action Party. After the leadership had contacted Lanciotto's widow in Campi Bisenzio to vouch for his identity, Stuart was appointed Area Commander in the centre of Chianti country. He was responsible for a mixed force of ex-prisoners of war and Italians and for liaison with the Communist partisan groups, and he described these months as some of the best of his life. The formation had a clear military line of command and only came together for specific operations such as sabotage, attacking a German unit, or receiving airdrops—the first of which was carried out in May.

On 27 June, Stuart was ordered into Siena to act as liaison officer when the city fell to the Allies. He walked in carrying a load of explosives and an identity card stating that he was an auxiliary policeman called 'Luigi Neri' and that he was allowed to carry arms. In the meantime, he was free to visit the sights of Siena. 'So I was on holiday,' Stuart recalled. The liberation of the city went smoothly and he was eventually repatriated by sea from Naples: 'Landfall with Blackpool tower just above the horizon. Four years before it had been my last sight of England.'

Stuart made several attempts to write a book about his time in Italy; in his view, all of his efforts failed. His memoir, *Pebbles from my Skull*, was published in 1963, but a new edition (with additional information) was released in 1985 as *Carlino*. The book was an attempt to describe what it had been like to live with the peasants and to record his gratitude to the large number of Italian men and women who had helped him. He also wanted to come to terms with his existential moment in the barn, when the possibility of survival had seemed remote, and also with his later experiences, when he had learned to apply the cruel logic of partisan warfare; he also had to make peace with the deaths on his conscience.

In particular, Stuart felt ready to answer the question: 'Why did it take me from September 1943 to 15 August 1944 to cross the line, resume my identity, step back out of limbo?' He related that there were half a dozen excuses to hand—ignorance, mistaken judgements, bad luck, the slowness of the Allied advance, the weather and the terrain. He was doing something for the war effort, and he had a responsibility to the escaped prisoners who turned to him for guidance; then there was a moral obligation to the Major and his group. All this was true, but it was irrelevant. What kept him in limbo was that he did not want to emerge from it.

Firstly, he was caught by a regression in time. Living with the Italians, he saw the last upsurge of peasant life and of an ancient civilization. Secondly, he was merely taking time out of life, escaping from war, which is itself an escape from reality. He added: 'Even this was not enough for me. I had to escape from the reality of war into something more romantic. A fugue within a fugue.' Finally, he dawdled because he liked it:

> There are moments in our lives when outward circumstances so exactly correspond to the inner structure of our being that our actions acquire an uncanny certainty ... Perhaps this conjunction gave the months I spent in Chianti their peculiar quality of happiness, overriding fear and the need to kill.[5]

Stuart related that in 1943 he was not shy but incredibly reserved. This was his defence against the world. However, in Chianti he became a member of a family and part of a conspiracy. He recalled: 'The currents of my life flowed together and swept me along. I wish their stream might have been more productive of human good, less costly in lives.'

In 1989 Stuart received an invitation from the Mayoress of Campi Bisenzio to join in the celebration of the anniversary of the liberation. He was made an honorary citizen for having taken an active part in the armed struggle as a partisan. To his surprise, the fight on the bare mountain had assumed a considerable importance in local history, and it was now known as the Battle of Valibona. It was said to be the first armed encounter in Tuscany between the partisans and the Fascist militia. The local Communist party had erected a stone on the hillside, and wreaths were regularly laid there. In the local branch of ANPI—the National Partisan Organization of Italy—there was a large portrait bust of Lanciotto and a photograph of the barn, surrounded by small images of those involved in the clash, with a space reserved for Stuart.

He discovered that there were local publications containing what one might call the 'authorised' version of the incident. In one of them, he found himself being described as involved in events that he was positive never took place, and others of which, if they did occur, he had no recollection. There were certain people whose reputation rested on their involvement, however marginal, in the activities of the partisan group; Stuart met one such man who claimed to have been involved in the action, who to Stuart's certain knowledge was not there. In short, what one might call the 'legend of Valibona' had evolved.

Stuart concluded his talk at Portsmouth University thus:

> The Battle of Valibona is interesting for a number of reasons. One is that it illustrates how opposing readings can attach to a moment in history. Another is that it raises the question of the accuracy of memory and the validity of interpretations of an event, whether at the time or in retrospect, by a person involved. It touches on the evolution of what I have called a legend—a narrative elaborated over the years in which many people are involved and in which some have a stake. It illustrates some of the problems attached to the historiography of the Italian Resistance which for too long was uncritical, too much given to celebrating martyrdoms, too reluctant to face up to errors and unnecessary deaths. The Italian Resistance had over 45,000 dead, among them Lanciotto Ballerini, who fought and died with the courage that posthumously earned him the Gold Medal of the Resistance.

Stuart was awarded the MBE for the actions he took during the period from his exit from PG 49 Fontanellato to his re-joining the Allied forces. During a career as a television executive, academic and writer, he remained a man of the left. He remarked, 'If I go back to Tuscany, I ask myself, "Well, was it worth it? To establish all these holiday homes?" … On the other hand, Fascism lost.'

8

The Free Zone of Ossola

Private Victor Ernest Walker (from Battersea, London) was captured by the Germans at Gazala, Libya, on 2 June 1942. He was serving as a driver with 157th Field Regiment, Royal Artillery. At the time of the 1943 Armistice, age twenty-four, he was part of a work detachment on the large plain west of Milan. The prisoners toiled all day in the rice fields on local farms, and in the evenings they returned to their camp at Ponzana—a satellite of PG 133 Novara.

On the night of 8 September, the Italian guards abandoned the camp, and in the morning the prisoners broke open the gates. The farmer said that they could remain and work for him, but this was not to be. Victor related that the next day, at around dinner time, while he was resting:

A local girl who worked on the rice farm came running out shouting: '*Tedeschi, Tedeschi*, the Germans are coming!' I immediately put my boots on and ran into the maize fields, which at this time of year were very tall and thick. I came to a stream. Some of the prisoners jumped across, but I fell in and lay under a bush. I heard the German soldiers firing on the prisoners and saw some of them go down, but did not know if they had been shot or not. I stayed under the bush all night and then proceeded upstream. I walked for between two to four days. I was tired, hungry, cold and very bewildered. I came to a road over the stream and was prepared to give myself up to the Germans.

I managed to scramble on to the road and saw a hay cart coming towards me with two men on it. I put my hands up in the air to surrender. The pair were Mario Baldi and his son, Domenico. They turned out to be farmers from Galliate. I tried to explain to them that I was an escaped prisoner of war and that I wished to give myself up. The men did not understand at first, as I could not speak much Italian. After a time they seemed to comprehend and beckoned to me to get under the hay in the cart. They covered me over and took me to their home.[1]

Victor suffered from malaria and was nursed by Mario and his wife, Pierina. The couple told their friends that he was a disbanded Italian soldier and provided him with a cap, coat and trousers to conceal his fair hair and appearance. When his health improved, Victor was given a bicycle. He dug and ploughed on the farm alongside Domenico, who had served with the fire brigade in Rome and was wanted by the Fascists. There were also two soldiers from Sicily at the farm; they had been cut off in the north by the Armistice. The fugitives lived in a small house that had a secret room and a large pipe through one wall to allow a quick escape into the fields. Mario and Pierina brought them food and washed their clothes. Victor was able to go into the village, and even to the cinema with Domenico, but he became very anxious when he realised that most of the audience were German and Italian troops.

The Baldi family were being watched by the Fascists, who suspected them of sheltering prisoners of war from the camp. On 16 September Victor and Mario were in the countryside, helping Domenico to look for a British prisoner of war he had met a few days earlier. Domenico left his companions, but after a few minutes they heard him cry out; he had been intercepted by a group of Fascists with shotguns and a dog. Domenico fired a pistol shot at the animal as it chased after him. One of the militiamen caught up with the farmer and beat him to the ground. Another Fascist aimed his revolver at Domenico's head and pulled the trigger; he managed to dodge the bullet, but he was left with a wounded hand. In the meantime, Mario arrived on the scene and scattered the enemy with musket fire, saving his son's life.

As a result of this incident the Fascists were on the trail of the three men. 'Conditions were getting very difficult,' Victor recalled. 'During the following week the three of us left Galliate to join the partisans, so that I would be able to get into Switzerland, even if it took a long time.'

Mario's wife and their daughter, Aurelia, remained in the village. However, a few days later their ration card was confiscated. The Blackshirts raided the house one evening, but the two women had been warned and had already fled. They lived in the countryside for two months and discovered that their home had been looted and razed to the ground.

After leaving Galliate, Victor, Mario and Domenico walked north to Lake Orta, took a boat, and crossed to Ronco on the western shore. They joined partisans in the mountains above Quarna. The detachment was composed of disbanded Italian soldiers and young Communists and was led by artillery captain Filippo Beltrami, who had been a Milanese architect in peacetime. The group became well-known to the people and to the Fascists, and it attracted prominent resistors—including Gianni Citterio, representative of the CLNAI in Milan; Gaspare Pajetta, a student and younger brother of Gian Carlo Pajetta, a member of the Communist military high command; and Alberto Li Gobbi, parachuted into Piedmont by the Allied secret services.

Victor was given a rifle, a bandoleer and ammunition, and a supply of hand grenades. The men were split into small groups. Sometimes there were Germans in villages they had to pass through. The partisans would attack at night, using their superior firepower, and retreat back into the hills, where the enemy would not follow them. Often the only drink was melting snow. The food was a spoonful of sugar a day and anything else that could be scavenged from Alpine huts that were abandoned in winter. When they were on the march, all the men suffered from frostbite to their hands and feet.

On 1 November, Victor was part of a detachment that trekked over the mountains to Lake Maggiore and attacked a small fort at Gravellona Toce. They stormed the army barracks and seized the rifles and ammunition. At the end of the month, the brigade marched through Omegna alongside the Communist partisans of Vincenzo Moscatelli.

In December the partisans returned to the Lake Orta area and raided another ammunition depot at Pogno. On the fourth of the month a mobile supply column led by Captain Beltrami was attacked by two Germans in a car at Borgomanero. The vehicle (with its *Wehrmacht* insignia) was seized, and its occupants were wounded. Two weeks later, the captain and his wife, Giuliana, were injured, and another partisan killed, when men from another band mistook them for Germans. That detachment was run by officer brothers Alfredo and Antonio Di Dio. Captain Beltrami decided that they should merge their forces in order to avoid such incidents in the future. The *Brigata Patrioti Valstrona* was created a few days later at Campello Monti.

In January 1944, after being attacked at Omegna, the guerrillas moved into the Ossola Valley, which links the western shore of Lake Maggiore and Switzerland. Meanwhile, Alfredo Di Dio was arrested when on a mission to Milan. A meeting was arranged for 13 February to prepare a plan of defence for the valley. The venue was a stone hut among chestnut woods, fifteen minutes' walk above the village of Megolo on the River Toce. The partisans awoke to find Megolo on fire and a superior German force advancing up the slopes. Captain Beltrami, Gianni Citterio, Antonio Di Dio, Gaspare Pajetta and eight other partisans were slain in two hours of fighting. In the months ahead, resistance was continued by an apolitical detachment known as the *Primo Gruppo Patrioti Filippo Beltrami*, which was formed by one of the captain's men, *Alpini* Lieutenant Bruno Rutto, with the assistance of Alfredo Di Dio, who escaped from Novara gaol in March.

Trekking over snow-covered peaks, Victor's group reached Malesco, where they fought another battle with the Germans. The enemy had encircled the base of the mountain. To escape their clutches the men had to flee through snow and ice, over rough tracks, until they reached Craveggia in the Vigezzo Valley. During the second week of April 1944, a guide found a suitable route into Switzerland for the men over the Spluga Pass. A group of seven partisans, including Victor and Domenico, approached a Swiss frontier guard. He contacted his officer by telephone, and afterwards told Victor that he could enter the country but his companions could not:

> I said I would go back with them, but they pleaded with me to think of my mother. The sentry took their ammunition from them and they went away. I think this was in case they used it to force their way in. I was escorted to the officer, who spoke English. He asked if I would like some coffee and a cigarette. I could not believe my eyes after so long without a proper drink. I was taken to a place where all my hair was shorn off and I was given a decent uniform to wear. My particulars were taken and I was informed that my name would be broadcast, with confirmation that I was safe and well.[2]

Victor joined other escaped Allied prisoners of war for rest and recuperation at the ski resort of Adelboden. After a couple of months, they were moved to a church hall at Elgg and allowed to take casual employment on local farms. Victor was delighted to receive a letter from his Italian friends, who said that that they too had eventually managed to cross the border. Together with all the other prisoners of war in the Confederation, he was repatriated following the Allied invasion of southern France in August 1944, which provided a land corridor.

In the months following Victor's departure from the Ossola Valley, there was a large influx of young volunteers who had rejected the RSI's call up. The rebels won control of vast areas of the countryside, also sabotaging railway lines and power installations, causing shut downs in industries in Novara and Milan. The Germans and Fascists responded with savage roundups, massacres and imprisonment.

In the summer the CLNAI in Milan adopted a plan for a partisan offensive, encouraged by the Allied onslaught and the capture of Rome. The scheme was promoted by military committee member Giovanni Battista Stucchi. For four months he acted as a delegate to the liberation committee in Lugano, Switzerland, and established close relations with the Allied secret agencies. There were strong partisan formations around Lake Orta—the *Filippo Beltrami* brigade in the Strona Valley, and the second *Garibaldi* division of tough and pragmatic Vincenzo Moscatelli (Cino) and his friend, Eraldo Gastone (Ciro), in the Sesia Valley. At the beginning of August the Germans were forced to agree to a neutral zone around Omegna due to persistent attacks by these forces. Across the River Toce in Ossola was the *Valtoce* Division, led by tank officer Alfredo Di Dio, whose younger brother, Antonio, had been slain at Megolo. To the east was the *Valdossola*, commanded by Major Dionigi Superti—a former airman and director of a logging firm. His men were deployed among the rugged mountains of the Val Grande and had already received airdrops of weapons and supplies from the Allies. Near the Swiss border, in the Cannobina Valley, was the *Piave*, led by Officers Armando Calzavara (Arca) and Filippo Frassati (Pippo), who were already known to the Allies through their help to escaped prisoners of war.

Two weeks before the start of the revolt, the partisans sent a representative for discussions with John McCaffery, head of the SOE in Switzerland. Colonel Attilio Moneta was middle-aged, lean, and grey-haired, with a bristling moustache. The British agent did not want to encourage the liberation of zones that could not be defended later; however, once it became clear that the partisans could not be stopped, he and the OSS chief in Switzerland, Allen Dulles, did everything they could to ensure the partisans received the support they needed. The Foreign Office voiced its disapproval from London. Max Corvo, head of OSS SI operations in Italy, also recalled that the plan was not presented to their agency:

> If it had been, the advice would have been negative, because it is axiomatic that irregular forces should not attempt to hold terrain against orthodox forces. Furthermore, the area in question had no particular significance to impending AAI operations which were aimed ultimately in the opposite direction toward Austria and southern Germany.[3]

The campaign began in the last week of August. Isolated garrisons in the mountains were overrun and the Cannobina Valley was freed. The railway lines south and east of Domodossola were cut and part of the system was operated by the partisans, using state employees and rolling stock.

Lieutenant George Paterson, a twenty-five-year-old Canadian attached to the British Army, was sent as the liaison officer. A native of Kelowna, British Columbia, he had been a forestry student at Edinburgh University on the outbreak of the war. George took part in the first commando raid in Italy—Operation Colossus—in February 1941. Eleventh SAS Battalion destroyed the Tragino Aqueduct, but the entire party was captured shortly afterwards. Following the 1943 Armistice, the Lieutenant escaped from a train near the Swiss border and helped the Resistance evacuate other Allied fugitives to Switzerland. He was recaptured early in 1944 by the Fascists and handed over to the SS. The Canadian broke out of the San Vittore prison in Milan after bribing a guard, and he was eventually spirited over the Swiss border by the escape organisation.

George was recruited by SOE Berne two or three days after the revolt began. John McCaffery told him:

'At the moment the partisans are all right for weapons, but if it starts to roll and recruits swarm in we'll have to get arms, ammunition and supplies to them by airdrop. That's one of the reasons why I need a man like you right on the spot.'

'There's another?' queried Paterson.

'Yes, this one is political. I don't know whether you realise it but these few square miles are the first in Italy to be free and under their own control for more than twenty years. A whole generation has grown up under Mussolini and since his fall we call the tune in the south and the Germans in the north, with this one exception. How are they going to handle themselves? Will they cooperate to govern or will they break up into factions with the possibility of civil war? This may give us some clue as to what will happen in the country as a whole once Jerry is finished.[4]

The Lieutenant was provided with a false identity card and dog tags in the name of an escaped prisoner of war, Major George Robertson of the Royal Engineers. At his request, he took Corporal Jack Watson with him as radio operator. Watson had been second in command of his section during Operation Colossus, and they had met again at the Swiss quarantine centre at Bad Lostorf. The pair were sent to Locarno. About a week later, McCaffery's subordinate, Major John Birbeck (himself an escaped prisoner of war), drove them to the border.

Three partisans were waiting on the other side. Their leader greeted George by saying, 'Let me welcome you to Free Italy. I'm Colonel Moneta, formerly of the Royal Sardinian Cavalry, and I am to be your liaison officer with our partisan brigades.' The agents were taken 2 miles to the Italian's home village of Malesco to meet the partisan leaders—Dionigi Superti, Alfredo Di Dio and Armando Calzavara. There was one notable absentee; Vincenzo Moscatelli had sent word that he was too busy to attend.

Over the next two weeks the partisans advanced southwards, averaging 3 or 4 miles on a good day. The soldiers in the isolated German garrisons in their path showed little appetite for a fight. Their equipment was taken and they were bundled over the Swiss border. George was surprised at the lack of enemy response, and every day he expected to hear that a fighting battalion had moved into the area. When this did not happen, he guessed that all the frontline troops were trying to stem the Allied advance from the south. During lulls in the fighting, the Lieutenant visited the partisan formations. He finally met Vincenzo Moscatelli and was impressed by his drive and determination, but he also noted that 'his force, like the others, lacked trained officers and NCOs, and was equally disorganised and unpredictable'.

By 1 September most of the land north of Domodossola was under

Resistance control. The rebels now forced the surrender of the garrisons crowded along the western shore of Lake Maggiore. On 8 September, coordinated attacks were launched on the few strong points and frontier posts still in enemy hands. In the morning, Domodossola was isolated and surrounded by 3,000 partisans, some armed with 20-mm field guns. The small frontier town is at the entrance to the Simplon Tunnel, on the main route from Milan to Berne, and the junction for a narrow gauge line to Ascona and Locarno in Switzerland.

The garrison consisted of 500 German and Italian troops (mostly SS). A combative priest called Don Luigi Zoppetti urged the partisans to make the town the capital of a liberated zone, from which the national uprising would radiate. The senior cleric, Don Luigi Pellanda, convened talks between the two sides. The leaders of the *Beltrami* Brigade and the two Communist divisions were excluded from the negotiations. The German and Italian commanders offered to remove their forces provided they would not be disarmed. They also said they would not leave without the Fascist administrators and their families. On behalf of the partisans, Dionigi Superti and Alfredo Di Dio agreed to allow the departure of the Germans with unloaded sidearms, but made the Fascists give up all their weapons. The confiscated items were stashed in a barracks, ready for use by the Resistance.

At dawn on Sunday 10 September, a long column of German and Italian vehicles prepared to leave Domodossola. The partisans checked for heavy weapons and gave permission for the convoy to leave for Fondotoce under escort. The Prefect of Novara, Enrico Vezzalini, told an angry Mussolini that 'not one shot was fired' in the defence of the town. As the enemy left, the partisans entered, welcomed by the ecstatic population. A proclamation was read out to inaugurate the Free Zone of Ossola; it covered 1,600 square kilometres (71 per cent of the present province of Verbano-Cusio-Ossola), with a population of about 75,000 living in thirty-five communes. Professor Ettore Tibaldi, a mild-mannered surgeon in exile in Switzerland, returned by special train to become president. The unfolding drama was relayed to the world press by dozens of foreign journalists who flocked across the border. The Swiss government eventually granted diplomatic recognition to the new zone, and a veteran anti-Fascist, Cipriano Facchinetti, became Ossola's ambassador in Berne.

Major Dionigi Superti, the leader of the Valdossola partisans, was entrusted with the task of creating a Provisional Governing Council—*la Giunta Provvisoria di Governo*. Housed in the *Palazzo di Città*, the assembly began an ambitious programme of reform based on democratic ideals. Dominated by party nominees, it claimed to receive its mandate from the local people to represent all the partisan formations, and to act according to the directives of the CLNAI. However, only two local liberation committees were established, and the people were never fully involved. The CLNAI were wary of the influence of their colleagues from the Swiss branch, and the *Beltrami* Brigade and the Communist formations were largely excluded from proceedings.

On 18 September the Governing Council introduced a daily bulletin; the political parties and even some of the partisan formations soon began to publish their own newspapers. Fascist laws and institutions were abolished, and new ministries were created overnight. Councils were re-established in the other communes and free trade unions were established. A Socialist lawyer, Ezio Vigorelli, became Minister of Justice. He introduced a legal system that safeguarded the rights of detainees, including the Fascist prisoners held at Druogno in the Vigezzo Valley. In the field of education, enrolment for 200 local schools began on 25 September, with a new term set to commence on 16 October. A commission was created to design a new curriculum.

While the politicians made ever more changes (including new street names), the people were more concerned with problems of survival. Rations were low, and there were shortages of money and basic necessities. Ten days after the occupation of Domodossola, only 500 litres of milk per day were available for the population of 14,000. Not even one sack of flour arrived from the plain, owing to the German blockade, and trains from Switzerland came loaded with political exiles but not foodstuffs. Fortunately, the Confederation did eventually agree to supply 200 quintals of potatoes a day on a commercial basis. A great deal of help was also provided by the Swiss and the Italian Red Cross organisations. The lack of finance was gradually alleviated by funds supplied by SOE and OSS, the minting of metal tokens by local industries, and the printing of paper coupons by the *Banca Popolare di Novara*, which were redeemed by the new Italian Republic after the war. The stock of RSI postage stamps was overprinted '*CLN—Ossola Libera—10.9.1944*'.

The partisans expelled more Fascist garrisons along the mouth of the River Toce, but the enemy still held the surrounding mountains. The rebels constructed three lines of defensive positions in this sector. Further north, the resort of Cannobio, near the Swiss border, changed hands several times. A local militia was created, led by Colonel Moneta. General Bianchi, the Italian military attaché in Berne, sent down a number of officers who had crossed the border on the 1943 Armistice and had been interned. On 18 September a Council of War was established, though it never functioned effectively due to political differences and clashes of personality. A deputation arrived from the CVL, headed by General Cadorna. He insisted on the need for a coordinated plan of defence and a unified command, even offering to take on leadership himself. This was rejected by the Communists. However, the decision was made to transform the Council of War into a Supreme Command. A three-times-decorated officer of the Italian Lancers from Cuneo, with the alias of 'Colonel Delle Torri'—real name Giuseppe Curreno di Santa Maddalena—was appointed Chief of Staff.

The Italians believed that an Allied airborne division could be dropped as a bridgehead for the final drive from the south. Two airfields were built for the landing—one at Santa Maria Maggiore in the Val Vigezzo, and another near Domodossola. However, they were never used. An airborne landing was planned for an earlier liberated zone—Montefiorino in Emilia—though it had to be cancelled at the last minute. Despite this, a similar initiative was never on the cards for its northern equivalent.

A letter sent by John McCaffery to Ferruccio Parri of the National Liberation Committee on 27 September reveals the real British attitude to the rising:

> You must not now claim to direct military operations in place of Alexander and Eisenhower. Some time ago I told you that the greatest military contribution you could make to the Allied cause was continuous, widespread sabotage on a large scale. You wanted to form armed bands. I approved your desire because I knew the value in morale of this for Italy. The partisans have fought well. We know this. But you have wanted to form armies. Who has asked you to do so? Not us.

Once Domodossola was captured, George witnessed chaotic meetings of the Governing Council:

> No one had any money to feed more than three thousand very hungry partisans. Cattle and supplies were commandeered, much to the annoyance of the peasant farmers and civilian members of the council, while the Professor, caught in the middle, had increasing difficulty in keeping the various factions from each other's throats.[5]

At one such meeting, the Canadian decided to take a trip back to Locarno. He told the assembly, 'It will be quicker that way to arrange airdrops of weapons and ammunition, and I can tell them that we desperately need money to pay for supplies.'

Professor Tibaldi replied, 'Impress on them that a government without money is like a well without water.'

George crossed the border, contacted Major Birbeck in Locarno, and returned the next day with 20 million lire and a precious schedule of airdrops on a typed sheet of onion skin. When the Lieutenant officially handed over the currency to Professor Tibaldi in Domodossola, he found himself the hero of the hour. Even Vincenzo Moscatelli congratulated him at this token of good faith on the part of Russia's allies.

The partisan leaders were also delighted at the opportunity to boost their firepower. The *Piave* Division were to receive the first consignment in three days' time. On the night of 10 October, George joined Armando Calzavara and a dozen of his men on a flat-topped hill north of Domodossola to await the consignment. Some German activity had been reported in the south, and the agent wanted to get the equipment and ammunition into partisan hands as quickly as possible. The sky was clear and serene, but as the appointed hour came and went no throb of aircraft engines broke the silence.

George apologised to Calzavara, but he only laughed and said, 'If things ever went right in this war, then we would really be concerned. Let's go back to town and have breakfast. We will try again three nights from now.'

The reason for the delay in the mission was flooding of the airfield of Celone in southern Italy. When flights were fully able to resume on 12 October, fifteen Liberator Mark VI bombers of the South African Air Force (SAAF) were sent to three drop zones in Piedmont, and five went to another target in Liguria. They arrived in the early evening.

Five aircraft from 31 Squadron were sent to a pinpoint codenamed 'Chrysler' in the lower Toce Valley, to the north-west of Lake Orta. South African Captain Bill Senn piloted Liberator KH 205 Y. The plane broke cloud immediately above an enormous black cross marked in the snow by the waiting partisans. The supplies went down, swaying at the ends of small parachutes. The plane returned to Celone at 10.50 p.m. after a round trip of six and a half hours. Twenty-five minutes later, the only other plane to make a successful drop on Chrysler arrived—EW 158 G, captained by Australian Flying Officer Max Badham, with an RAF crew. He reported that weather and visibility were poor, with low cloud and lightning over the target. Many lights were flashing, but the correct pattern was not discernible; however, the local topography was positively identified. The supplies were released and all the parachutes were seen to open. The officer was a big man, and so he was able to handle the unwieldy Liberator in the strong currents of wind that threatened to push the planes into the mountains.

Another aircraft, KH 104 F, flown by South African Lieutenant Cyril Le Sueur, reached the north Italian coast, but when its bomb doors were tested it was found that they could not be completely opened. The plane returned to base with its contents.

The other two Liberators assigned to Chrysler crashed in high mountains to the south-west, with the loss of all those on board. KG 875 D, flown by South African Captain Leonhard von Solms Beukes, age twenty-six, was found at Valprato Soana; KG 999 P, piloted by his compatriot, Lieutenant Charles Nel, age twenty-one, crashed at Ala di Stura. In total, forty-eight airmen belonging to the air forces of South Africa, the United Kingdom and Australia were lost on the one night of 12 October 1944.

There would be no further supply drops to the liberated zone; a counter-offensive had begun. It was led by German SS General and Police Major-

General Willy Tensfeld, liaison officer to the Fascists. His task force included 500 of his countrymen, but it was mainly composed of detachments from the National Republican Army and auxiliaries of the locally recruited Black Brigade, the *6th Augusto Cristina* of Novara. About 5,000 partisans were outmanned and outgunned in every sector where they opposed the enemy, and they were forced to fall back to new positions in the mountains.

After some diversionary thrusts from the south on 11 October, the main attack began in the north. Colonel Moneta roused George with the news during the night:

> 'Word has just come down from Malesco that a whole German battalion, Alpine troops, and some Fascist infantry, have got across Lake Maggiore and landed near Cannobio. We had a patrol in the area and they could do nothing but fall back into the mountains. They blew the bridge through the pass and that may slow the Germans down a little. Di Dio is up there, assembling his brigade at Malesco, and he's going to move forward at dawn to try and halt them in the pass. If we don't stop them there, they'll be in behind us along the frontier and then....' He drew a finger across his throat expressively.[6]

A car was found and George drove the Colonel and Corporal Watson the 30 miles to Malesco. They arrived soon after first light, but the partisans had already marched out in the direction of Finero. The Corporal was instructed to stay in Malesco; if things went wrong, he was to return to Switzerland and tell Major Birbeck.

The Lieutenant drove on until he reached a long, straggling column of 500–600 men. They were the zone's mobile reserve, formed from one of the two brigades of the *Valtoce* and reinforcements from the *Piave*. The guerrillas told the Canadian that Commandant Di Dio and his officers had driven ahead to reconnoitre the bridge destroyed by their forces the previous evening.

When George caught up with the leaders, they asked if he would like to go along. He agreed because he feared that any hesitation on his part might be misinterpreted. However, the agent thought it was folly for the officers to push on so far ahead, particularly as the mission was best undertaken by a scouting patrol. '*In bocca al lupo*,' ('Good luck,'), he replied. In English, this Italian expression translates as 'In the mouth of the wolf'. The 1967 book narrating George's experiences (written by John Windsor, a blind Canadian veteran of the war in Italy) would be entitled *The Mouth of the Wolf*.

Ten of the men piled into two cars and drove for a mile across an open valley. They came to a line of low mountains and walked the last 500 yards to the bridge. As they discussed plans to surprise the advancing Germans, it suddenly became apparent that it was they who had fallen into a trap:

All hell broke loose. From somewhere high on the ridge heavy machine guns stuttered into life. It was so unexpected that for seconds they just sat, confused by the mounting crescendo of noise as echoes began to multiply and re-multiply the sound. Then they saw the distant column disintegrate into a multitude of running figures as the fire tore into the ranks and the men dived for safety.[7]

The two Fiats were hit and their petrol tanks exploded. A culvert under the road provided the only shelter; George and some of the Italians managed to dash to safety, but Alfredo Di Dio was cut down in the attempt. When the enemy finally rushed the position after two hours, Colonel Moneta was also slain. The Lieutenant had run out of ammunition and threw his tommy gun down. Angry Germans began to kick and punch him, and he passed out after a rifle butt caught him across the head. When the Canadian came round, he faced two soldiers who had cocked their rifles for his summary execution. A sergeant major yelled at them to stop—prisoners were to be taken for interrogation.

On 13 October the Italian infantry, backed up by armoured train from Baveno, scattered the main partisan force in the lower Toce valley. At 5.40 p.m. the following day, enemy troops re-entered Domodossola. The streets were almost deserted as more than half the population had fled. Three special trains had taken hundreds of civilians and partisans across the border to Ascona. The refugees were sent to Basle and on to camps in central Switzerland. The final clashes took place along the frontier on 23 October. After only forty-three days, the liberated zone was no more.

At first, George was sent to Novara gaol. He managed to have a letter smuggled out to Major Birbeck, which read in part: 'It was partly my own fault getting caught. Let my natural instinct be overridden by a burst of Italian enthusiasm.' The Lieutenant was then returned to the San Vittore gaol in Milan, and once again fell into the clutches of the SS.

A few hundred partisans evaded the enemy and gradually resumed military operations. On 24 April 1945, the Resistance finally liberated the Ossola zone and moved into western Lombardy. Four days later, Milan, 'Capital of the Resistance,' was freed. At 1 p.m., the Communist divisions entered the city led by a shiny, black open touring car and seven captured tanks. Among the crowd was the SOE agent George Paterson, newly released from prison. The Canadian suddenly realised that the man waving from the rear of the car was Vincenzo Moscatelli. The Communist leader saw him at almost the same instant, and, shouting to his driver to stop, he jumped out and rushed over. '*Giorgio,*' he beamed, shaking hands enthusiastically. 'I thought the worms had you months ago. This is a surprise, and on such a great day for Italy.

Come along, you've got to ride with me. You should be in the parade. I want to hear your story.'

For his work with the Resistance, George Paterson was promoted to Captain and awarded the Military Cross with two bars. He was also made an honorary citizen of Milan—an honour rarely bestowed on foreigners.

9

Bravery in the Field

William 'Bill' Pickering was born in Oldham, Lancashire, in 1923. He was working as a junior clerk for a grocery chain when the Second World War began. A true patriot, Bill volunteered to join the British Army in 1940 at the age of seventeen, altering his birth certificate by one year to hide the fact he was underage. In 1987, at Bologna University, he told a commemorative conference of ex-SOE agents and partisans:

> Little did I realise at that time that I would one day marry an Italian girl and that I would eventually be fighting on the Italian side, helping to drive the German Nazis out of Italy. After some time in the infantry I volunteered for SOE in early 1942 and was accepted by them before my nineteenth birthday and was trained as a radio operator. After serving in North Africa and Sicily I had the good fortune to become part of No. 1 Special Force, a unit in which Max Salvadori was an officer. I was selected as his operator on the Anzio beachhead landing where we tried to get through the German lines with Alberto Tarchiani. Unfortunately, our mission had to be evacuated due to death, injury and illness among our small group and I found myself in Monopoli helping to run the SOE base signal station there. Shortly afterwards I was delighted to hear that Max wanted me to act as his radio operator once more on a mission to be parachuted into the Piedmont area early in 1945.

On 4 February, the SOE Chariton Mission parachuted from an American Dakota (based at Cecina) into the snow-covered, rolling hills of the Langhe in southern Piedmont. Max and Bill were accompanied by four other agents: South African Major Adrian Hope, Irish Captain John Keany, English Corporal 'Busty' Millard, and American radio operator 'Giovanni', who soon left to join other OSS agents.

Max, Bill and John were to go to Milan to liaise with the CLNAI. Adrian was to lead a secondary mission to the autonomous partisan brigade at Cisterna d'Asti, with 'Busty' as his radio operator. The formation, which later developed into the Sixth Alpine Division '*Alpi*', was led by Giovanni Toselli (Otello). The agents' main priority would be to ensure an orderly takeover when the Germans fled or surrendered. The pair were later joined by Roman lawyer Luigi Cavalieri (Roccia), who would act as their translator. The reception committee was headed by another South African SOE agent, Captain Hugh Ballard.

Bill recalled that their party of six made a safe landing in the Val Bormida, close to the village of Monesiglio:

> It was there that I first came into contact with Major Enrico Mauri and his autonomous group of well-organised partisans. I was particularly impressed by the way in which they handled our drop and very quickly moved our group, together with the large quantity of arms and ammunition we had dropped with us. Everything was very well hidden in the vaults of a local church in a very short time before the German SS troops came looking for us. Once more I was impressed by the speed and efficiency with which we were spirited into the surrounding countryside.

The party divided and the men were taken to local farms. Bill and John were sheltered by Tal and Luisa Biestro on their holding just outside the village of Monesiglio:

> This was to be the first of many examples of the Piedmont country people assisting our mission to achieve its aim. We slept in the house overnight and every day, just as dawn was breaking, we would move into a small wooden shed about two hundred yards above the house where the farmer's wife would cover us with dry leaves. She would come up twice a day to bring us food, almost in sight of the German garrison, taking terrible risks to make sure that we were well looked after. Every evening after dark we would come down to the farmhouse and operate the radio from the attic, transmitting messages to our base in southern Italy. Many of the neighbours had their houses burnt down and their menfolk killed for such acts, but this did not deter the farmer and his wife in any way from helping us to rid Italy of the enemy.

Captain John Keany, age thirty, was a public-school-educated Catholic from County Cork, in the neutral Irish Free State. He volunteered to serve in the Irish Fusiliers on the outbreak of war and took part in the conquest of Italian East Africa. Bill remembered his friend thus:

[He was] a powerfully built man in his prime, standing five feet ten inches tall, with brown hair and blue eyes ... He was courageous to a fault, wanting to fight and engage the enemy at every opportunity. He had a terrific sense of humour and was the life and soul of our party.

Bill related that Max soon left to make his way to Milan. After a lying low for few nights, the rest of the group began their journey to Cisterna d'Asti:

There were six in the party: myself, John Keany, Major Adrian Hope, 'Busty' Millard, Roccia, and our guide, Settimo Maggiorino, a member of the *Alpini*, who was to turn out to be such a great friend and first class guide, as well as being an extremely good soldier. He led us to the River Tanaro, about one hundred yards from the bridge at Alba where a group of partisans had organised a regular crossing by the use of ropes to pull the boats across under the noses of the German sentries on the bridge. We managed to cross successfully and continued on to Cisterna d'Asti, where we were to meet Colonel Otello and his active and enthusiastic group of partisans. After spending a couple of days there I set off with John Keany to walk across country to Milan where we were to meet Max Salvadori once again.

The agents were given peasant clothes and floppy hats to pull over their battle dress, but the disguise was rather spoiled by the army boots that they insisted on keeping. The pair set off with a donkey and cart for an appointment with a group of Justice and Liberty partisans near German-occupied Villanova. At around midnight, as they entered the little town, there was a massive explosion and a blinding flash lit the sky. Another group of rebels had blown up a train. The agents fled the scene as quickly as the donkey could carry them, but suddenly a voice shouted out of the darkness, 'Stop! Put your hands in the air!' The pair gradually made out the red neckerchiefs and brigand uniforms of a heavily armed *Garibaldini* patrol. Only British Gold Flake cigarettes and Captain Keany's promise of a lavish supply airdrop persuaded the suspicious Communists to let them go on their way.

As arranged, the agents rendezvoused on the margins of the town with Gino Paltrinieri (Gino), second in command of the Justice and Liberty partisan group, who led a force of 120 men. He was to take the soldiers to his commandant, 'Renato'. In turn, he would guide them north to Brusasco. There they would seek out Doctor Ferrero Burrino, a partisan sympathiser, who would drive them to Milan in his car.

'Gino' led the two agents to 'Renato' in the Montafia area on the morning of 8 March. Captain Keany wanted to press on to Brusasco, but the Italian commander said that the journey would be safer by night. It was also necessary to disperse the bulk of the force from the open hillside. In the end, it was agreed that 'Renato' and a group of twenty men would stay with the agents; they would move off when the coast was clear. However, as 'Gino' led the rest of the partisans away at 9 a.m., Bill noticed German troops entering a farmhouse on the hillside a mile below them. He recalled that the enemy managed to creep up the slope, unseen, over the next two hours:

> Unfortunately, my colleague John Keany was killed in the first burst of fire from the SS troops who had virtually surrounded us on a hilltop. Most of the partisans had left us an hour earlier, and I had my most impressive view of their comrades in action. Although under enemy fire, they fought their way out in a most orderly and gallant fashion. Heavily outnumbered, the partisans took it in turn in small groups of three or four to get down and give covering fire while their comrades retired, and they, in their turn, would engage the Germans until we had all extricated ourselves from what had been a very precarious situation. We lost four or five men in this action, but my radio set was intact and the rest of us were alive to continue our fight against the occupiers. What had struck me most was the coolness of 'Renato' and his brave comrades, who never at any time panicked, just fighting their way out of the trap and living to continue their superb resistance.

After the war it was revealed that the partisan commander with the alias of 'Renato' was an American OSS agent. His real name was Riccardo Vanzetti, and he was an engineer and lieutenant in the Italian Royal Air Force. He had been parachuted in as second in command to fellow airman Marcello De Leva, of the Secret Intelligence Orange Mission, in March 1944. According to the Americans, Riccardo showed 'a superior aptitude for irregular warfare'. He assumed command of the Justice and Liberty partisans in the Monferrato area and organised squads to attack enemy communications and installations. The agent was given increasing levels of responsibility as leader of a unit known as the Mobile Operational Group, which stormed into Turin in the final offensive.

Bill lacked orders after the loss of his comrade, and he had no way of reaching Milan or returning to Allied lines. He decided to join the secondary mission led by Major Hope, and to share the duties of radio operator with 'Busty'. The Major was a forty-seven-year-old South African advocate and veteran of the First World War. He had already liaised with partisans in Greece and Yugoslavia. Bill remembered him as 'a quietly spoken colonial type who spoke to us in the clipped tones of the BBC announcers', adding that 'the partisans grew to love him'.

When he was not attending to his role as radio operator, Bill joined the partisans in their operations. He became known to them as 'English Billy' or 'Blondie':

I made my way back to Cisterna where I was to witness the tremendous efforts of Otello and his very active group, continually harassing the German and Italian Republican troops. Otello led a highly organised resistance unit which had good communications with other groups in Piedmont, enabling them to cooperate and carry out large-scale attacks on the enemy. Otello also had an intelligence network which worked extremely well and enabled his group to forestall many moves which were made against them by the enemy. He was ably assisted by a complete family, Gris and Grisa and their three sons, who took part in all operations.

These missions were very varied and must have been a real thorn in the side of the enemy, many raids being carried out with great nerve and audacity. They included attacks on the railway stations at San Damiano and Bra where many enemy were killed and large numbers of prisoners taken. At the same time, bridges were being blown up and vehicles ambushed. More weapons were being acquired from these raids, as well as those obtained from drops by Allied aircraft. Unfortunately, the British Liaison Officer, Major Hope, was killed at this time. He had been a source of inspiration to the partisans and was very well liked by everybody.

As April approached, the partisans became bolder and more confident. Some individuals showed amazing instances of bravery, dressing up as Fascist officers and going to the local railway station where they kidnapped German soldiers at gun point and brought them back to Cisterna as prisoners. At this time we were able to manage much larger drops from the Allied aircraft and increased our activities against the Germans who by now were becoming increasingly afraid of partisan raids. They would not venture out at night, thus allowing the partisans to move about and plan even more daring actions. All the resistance groups could now foresee that they would not have to wait very long for the liberation of the Italian cities.

The Military Committee of the Piedmont partisans had drawn up plans for the final offensive as early as February. Action began on 18 April with a general strike. Two days later, the committee told its commanders that the formations would first free their own zones, and then about 10,000 men would march on Turin to help in its liberation and to give support to Allied operations. Only on the arrival of this force would the signal for the rising within the city be given.

However, on 24 April the CLN learned that the Allies had crossed the River Po near Mantua. The rebels consulted the British Liaison Officer, Colonel John Stevens. He told them that the British and Americans would rapidly converge on the city from Genoa and Piacenza. As a result, the Liberation Committee issued its directive for a general rising, effective the next day. However, 15th Army Group opposed the order; they declared that it was untimely and dangerous given the presence of retreating German divisions in the area. The Colonel ordered the partisans not to leave their own operative zones. Bill recalled that the Allies gambled on their own forces reaching the city before the partisans:

> As the end of April approached at last the news came through that the Allies were attacking in a final push to end the war in Italy. I remember receiving a message from Allied Forces Headquarters that the partisans were to wait for the Allies to arrive and not to occupy any towns or cities. This request naturally fell upon deaf ears. The partisans were in no mood to take any notice of such an order. It was their country, they had been fighting and waiting for this day for far too long and were not going to be deprived of the pleasure of liberating their own towns and cities and chasing the enemy out themselves.
>
> Otello's group liberated Asti amid terrific scenes of joy and relief, the whole city turning out to welcome them. Then it was the turn of Turin to be liberated. The partisans requisitioned vehicles wherever they could get hold of them and poured into the city. Rifles and machine guns were rattling all around as fierce street fighting took place and bodies were lying everywhere. The German divisions were retreating as fast as they could go, having been well beaten by the partisans. When these divisions finally halted, they negotiated a surrender to Colonel Stevens to the north of Turin.

The truce concluded by the German garrison with the partisans in the hills at Tronzano Vercellese lasted until the arrival of the Allies on 1 May. The Liberation Committee were running the commune, public services were working, and the factories had been saved from destruction. On the same day, the 75th German Army Corps of General Ernst Schlemmer surrendered unconditionally in Biella to the partisan command and to Captain Patrick Amoore as representative of the SOE Cherokee Mission and the Allies:

> At last it was all over. The Italian partisans had triumphed, liberating their own country, preventing the economic disruption and scorched earth policy which the Germans had promised. These partisans had earned Italy its rightful place among the free nations of the world by their own magnificent efforts, and in doing so had proved that free men cannot be subjugated by tyrants and dictators. The example of the new partisan leaders who had taken up arms against the oppressors had lit the spark in those thousands of Italian patriots who had followed them until their country was free. I feel very proud to have taken part in a small way in this great re-awakening of the Italian spirit and I will be forever grateful for the experience and for the many lasting friendships I made among my Italian comrades in their moment of glory.

In October 1945, Bill was awarded the Military Medal for Bravery in the Field. The citation reads:

Sergeant Pickering was parachuted into south Piedmont on 4 February 1945 in company with the British senior representative to the CLNAI. After about ten days in the Langhe area during which time the party was continually chased by German troops, Sergeant Pickering, in company with one of the officers of this mission, set out in an attempt to reach the neighbourhood of Brusasco. They moved constantly through enemy infested country until they reached the area of Montafia when they were again subjected to an enemy drive. On 8 March 1945 they were forced to hide with a small partisan party on a hill in this area. Here they were attacked by the enemy in force and in the course of this action the officer with Sergeant Pickering was killed together with four partisans and the rest of the party was forced to withdraw. Sergeant Pickering risked his own life by continuing to carry the W/T set which he succeeded in saving from falling into enemy hands.

Sergeant Pickering remained in the area until he could recover the body of his officer and arrange for its burial. After that he made his way back through enemy infested country to join up with another British mission at Cisterna.

Bill was posted back to Italy after the war. In Florence, he met a beautiful *signorina* named Rossana Reboli. She was with her mother at a New Year's Eve dance in the sergeants' mess at the Villa San Camillo. By the time Bill was posted to Rome in March 1946, he and Rossana had become engaged. He visited Rossana again after being demobbed in 1947, and in October of that year they were married at St Chad's Roman Catholic Church in Cheadle, Cheshire.

Bill was reunited with his commanding officer, Lieutenant-Colonel Massimo ('Max') Salvadori, at the 1987 Bologna Conference. In his memoir, *The Bandits of Cisterna* (written with the journalist Alan Hart), Bill recalled the impression he had of his colleague when on the Chariton Mission:

Soldiers cannot elect their leaders, but I could think of nobody that I would have rather followed in such a situation ... Major Max was six feet tall, with brown hair and striking pale blue eyes. He sported a military moustache of the type favoured by Errol Flynn, Clark Gable and other Hollywood stars who represented the swashbuckling school of acting. He came from the Marche region of Italy, near Ancona, and had served a prison sentence prior to the outbreak of war because of his anti-Fascist views. Fluent in Italian, of course, the major also spoke impeccable English with an educated public school accent.[1]

Max Salvadori, age thirty-six in February 1945, belonged to the ancient Marche family of the counts of Salvadori-Paleotti. Born in London, he had an English grandmother and was brought up as a Protestant. In 1924, Max and his philosopher father, Guglielmo, were attacked by Fascist thugs in Florence. The family fled to Switzerland, where the young man graduated from the University of Geneva. He returned to Italy and took his doctorate at Rome University, but he was arrested in 1932 as a Justice and Liberty activist. Max was amnestied the following year after the intervention of an influential English cousin. He farmed in Kenya for another three years and then found employment in the United States as a lecturer in economics and sociology at St Lawrence University.

Max worked with British Intelligence in the Americas on the outbreak of war. In 1943 he was accepted as a commissioned officer in the British Army, and he joined SOE after an interview with Colonel Cecil Roseberry at their headquarters in Baker Street, London. Max landed in Sicily with the 8th Army and became a captain in Special Force's forward detachment, codenamed 'Vigilant', under the alias of 'Max Sylvester'. The detachment rescued the philosopher Benedetto Croce from Sorrento, but came to grief on the Anzio beachhead in February 1944. Bill was the captain's signalman on the mission. Max had to be evacuated owing to a bout of jaundice. He then took part in operations to insert agents into enemy territory and was awarded the Military Cross. His aptitude and knowledge of Italian politics soon ensured that he was made liaison officer to the emerging partisan movement and that he was eventually promoted to the rank of Lieutenant-Colonel.

Following the landing of the Chariton Mission in southern Piedmont on 4 February 1945, it took several weeks for Max to leave for his mission to the CLNAI, as he told the Bologna Conference:

> I reached Milan in the early morning of a cold and grey late winter day of 1945, one month after having been parachuted. I had been delayed by the usual difficulty of coordinating the movements of the four-man mission and of guides sent by the CLN with the aim of getting me as safely as possible to Milan, and by a lengthy *rastrellamento* carried out in February.

The instructions given to Max by Lieutenant-Colonel Richard Hewitt when he left No. 1 Special Force base were concise. The main points were to find out which formations needed help most, to plan through the CLNAI for the defence of industrial plant, and to make sure that CLNs at all levels were taking measures for the takeover of the administration when the enemy surrendered. In addition, German troops were to be treated as prisoners of war, the fate of armed Fascists was to be decided on by the CLN, and measures were to be taken to prevent looting and random acts of vengeance. Max recalled that the most important instruction was given orally by Commander 'Gerry' Holdsworth: 'Do your best!'

> Once in enemy territory the liaison officer (BLO) was on his own. Within the frame of general and vague instructions the BLO had as guide his knowledge and appreciation of the situation and his conscience. He had greater latitude than imagined by resistors accustomed to the rigid rules which are the norms in dictatorial systems. Politics? It was reiterated again and again that military considerations, the contribution to the Allied war effort, were the foremost concern.

Personal security and the lack of a radio were Max's immediate problems. He knew that the risk of clandestine operators being caught was at its greatest in urban areas. A young guide who brought him to Milan, Giordana, arranged for him to stay with a trusted friend and also provided him with a bicycle. Unknown to all except a member of the CLNAI, Max also had a base in the Bruzzano district. He related:

> 'No one knew that I made use of the apartment of a cousin I had not seen for over twenty years. I met many people but psychologically, as stated in *The Economist* of 16 February 1985 by Professor Foot, I was 'alone and always on the run'.

Communication with No. 1 Special Force remained a concern:

> Books tell of what was done and seldom mention failures. Keany and Pickering had been instructed to remain in uniform. In case of capture it made the difference between being a prisoner of war and being shot—as Newton had been in Sicily. It meant restricting their movements to areas controlled by partisans. Couriers would maintain contacts. None sent from Milan reached his or her destination. There was no news until I was notified that Keany had been killed in action near a locality of the Basso Monferrato ... The presence of an Allied radio soon became known among the Resistance, and Pickering linked partisans and CLN of the area with No. 1 Special Force base. I knew in Milan of four Allied radios, among them an ORI-OSS one in the city. They were all extremely cooperative. Couriers took the eight detailed reports I wrote during that period to the SOE representative in Lugano (helped by the Swiss Captain Bustelli).

Max met the political leaders of the five political parties in the CLNAI—the Communists, Socialists, Christian Democrats, Liberals and Actionists. He knew some of the men by reputation, while he had encountered others before in the south. Max was invited to attend meetings of the committee but only went once, when the capture of Mussolini was announced. Max took a legalistic view of the situation, as befitted an academic, explaining that in the interim period, before the arrival of the Allies, the CLNAI would exercise the delegated power of government, including the administration of justice. In such an exceptional moment it was up to them to decide which laws to apply. Within a few days of his arrival, Max had also met prominent members of the central military committee and partisan commanders. Altogether he saw about sixty Resistance personalities—a few only once, and several many times.

In March, a rising number of volunteers were flowing into the partisan formations, Moscatelli's Communist divisions were growing in strength in the Valsesia, and continual firing at night indicated that patriotic action groups were active in Milan. Members of the CLNAI told Max what was being done by the partisans to defend industrial plant and take over administration at the moment the enemy gave up the struggle. His conclusion was that there was evidence of efficiency, discipline and a sense of responsibility:

> The partisans would coordinate their operations with those of the Allies, the defeat of the Germans and the disintegration of the RSI would not be followed by chaos and a free for all in which the strongest—i.e. the most disciplined and best armed groups—would triumph. One could expect an orderly transition—in the circumstances more unique than rare.

The end came quickly:

> On the evening of 25 April it was all over, except for skirmishes I witnessed the following morning. I addressed the Italian nation over the Milan radio together with the spokesman for the CLNAI, the Actionist Riccardo Lombardi. Lieutenant-Colonel Vincent arrived and took charge. On 6 May, if I remember correctly, I accompanied members of the CLNAI to Rome. My mission was over.

Max was awarded the DSO by the British (to add to his earlier MC), and he was also made an honorary citizen of Milan by the Italians. In a report to Winston Churchill on the political situation in Italy, dated 13 June 1945, Sir Noel Charles, the British Ambassador, wrote that Max had participated actively in the work of the CLNAI for three months:

> As a former political prisoner of the Fascists he had the confidence of all parties and he did not hesitate to use his influence fully and courageously in preserving the unity of the committee and in securing the carrying out of their undertakings.

At the 1987 Bologna conference, Max made two speeches. One was entitled 'Mission to the CLNAI'. The other, 'Random Considerations on the Road to the CLNAI', provided valuable insights into the work of agents:

> Partisan urban guerrillas and CLN members in 1943–45, as well as Italian writers on the resistance ever since, have generally ignored the difficulties SOE had in establishing contacts and sending supplies. Academic scholars and armchair strategists should try to figure out step by step how action takes place. It was not easy to cross a battle front, whatever the means employed. A wireless set was not a bundle one could put under one's coat. In enemy territory it was not easy to find the people one was looking for, to find localities where supplies could be landed or dropped. It is easy to talk about destroying an enemy ammunition dump or bridge, it was difficult to do it. It was not easy to avoid the enemy, his collaborators and informers (Germans were not idle and their efficiency is often forgotten), to be aware of the duplicity of turncoats more interested in their factional goals than in winning the war, to recognise spies and double agents.
>
> Even before reaching Naples, thanks partly to ex-prisoners of war who had managed to cross enemy lines, and to rather vague news coming mainly through Switzerland, officers of the small SOE-operated unit commanded by Major Munthe which had participated in the Salerno landing, knew about large gatherings of disbanded soldiers, of young people avoiding German and Fascist conscription, and of evacuees in wooded hills and mountainous areas. How could they be contacted? Any British or Commonwealth officer and NCO would have been soon caught, and if in civilian clothing, shot straight away, as Lieutenant Newton had been in Sicily.
>
> A few Italians volunteered for blind landings and drops. Casualties were heavy and unreported. Of those contacted in enemy territory how many would be willing to blow up bridges and ammunition dumps, to ambush enemy personnel or to engage in the kind of subversion now called destabilization? Action necessitated ability to pass unobserved, self-control, quick reactions, firmness, patience and, if caught, endurance under torture. Of course, there were men and women willing to die (we all know how many died in those fateful twenty months), but they had to be found, and they had to be given the means with which to be able to engage in action.
>
> Everything took time, often a desperately long time. The Ancona CLN sent a courier on a small boat to contact the Allies, 200 miles to the south. Recognized as a bona fide combatant, he returned with instructions for receiving the supplies: it takes a few lines to write what took months! Not all the supplies reached their destination. The courier was killed.
>
> Instructions given to British Liaison Officers (BLOs) were summarised in eleven words: 'find who needs what and will make good use of it'. In

all countries in which SOE operated the BLO had to be a good judge of men, to distinguish between *attendisti* and *attivisti*, between those who would use the armament received and those who would store it; he had to endure loneliness, hunger and whatever the sky brought; he had to find his way in an unfamiliar maze. Not easy tasks. 'Men and women ... alone or in small numbers, deep inside enemy-held territory, giving aid to the indigenous resistance movements, and nearly always on the run.' This is how *The Economist* of 16 February 1985 described SOE officers and NCOs. Wirelesses failed, drops went astray. Errors made in France, Greece, the Netherlands and Yugoslavia had to be avoided. Courage was not enough. Once behind enemy lines the BLO was no longer an officer carrying out orders: he had no other guide than himself, his sense of duty and his perception of the situation.

At HQ not all requests could be satisfied. After the opening of two fronts in France and the changed attitude of Yugoslav partisans towards the Allies, the Italian front had become less than secondary. There was scarcity of everything from DC-3s to Sten guns to blankets. In November 1944 scarcity had reached the point that led the Commander in Chief, desirous of avoiding the tragedy that had befallen the Polish Home Army a few weeks earlier, to warn partisans of the difficult months ahead. Scrounging, the No. 1 Special Force Commanding Officer was able to keep the flow of supplies at a decent level.

What could be done, what—notwithstanding the difficulties—had to be done, was done. We did our best—always less than one wants, and often less than others expect. SOE officers died, and no publicity was given to their deaths. Others were wounded or captured. There were three operative officers when we went to Anzio. One died and one was badly wounded and never recovered [Captain Michael Gubbins and Major Malcolm Munthe]. There were again three when we were parachuted early in February 1945, on my way to Milan: two died [Major Adrian Hope of the South African Staff Corps and Captain John Keany, Royal Irish Fusiliers, Chariton Mission]. The war was won and this is what matters. Members of dozens of missions sent into enemy territory did better than any armchair expert in the armed resistance of 1943–45 would have done.

On leaving the Army, Max Salvadori lectured at Smith College in Northampton, Massachusetts, becoming Professor of Modern European History. Apart from short leaves of absence to fill senior roles in UNESCO and NATO, he taught there until his retirement in 1973.

10

Extra-Hazardous Duty with the OSS

British missions shared enemy territory in Italy with those of the United States Office of Strategic Services (OSS), the forerunner of the Central Intelligence Agency. The OSS was created out of William Donovan's Office of the Coordinator of Information (COI), which had opened a bureau on Grosvenor Street in Mayfair, London, in August 1941.

When President Roosevelt and the Joint Chiefs of Staff were signing the orders creating the OSS on 13 June 1942, its director, Colonel (later Major-General) Donovan, was in London, negotiating with SOE. The secret services agreed to cooperate in the field and to specify theatres of operations. Italy and Switzerland—among other countries—were to be shared. There would be no joint operations, but the separate missions would work out of an integrated headquarters in a spirit of friendly competition.

OSS in Italy had responsibility for the Mediterranean Theatre. It operated from a HQ at Caserta. The main branches working in Italy were Special Operations (SO), Secret Intelligence (SI), Counter-Intelligence (X-2), Morale Operations (MO), which covered only black propaganda, and the Operational Groups (OGs), which organised commando-style operations alongside the Italian partisans. The base for maritime and aerial activities was Brindisi, and the radio network was located in Bari. The Fifth Army detachment of SI was assigned a tactical role, while the Palermo station was given the task of strategically penetrating the parts of Italy north of Rome through parachute operations. An advance base was also set up on Sardinia, although it later moved to Corsica.

The operational groups of the OSS were composed of officers and enlisted men who volunteered for 'extra-hazardous duty behind enemy lines'. They were organised in small groups and parachuted into occupied territory to harass the enemy and to encourage and support local resistance organisations. At a 1994 Venice Conference on the Americans and the War of Liberation in

Italy, attended by veterans from the OSS and the Resistance, former senior liaison officer Emilio Caruso recalled:

> General Donovan had an idea. The United States had a vast number of first generation Americans of European parentage. This was especially true of the Italian-Americans whose parents were part of a large and most recent wave of immigration. Why not form fighting units of these hyphenated Americans, as he would often call them? Their family background and knowledge of the language would make them valuable fighters behind enemy lines. These were to be military units rather than intelligence operatives. And so the Operational Groups, OGs as they came to be known, were formed.

The Joint Chiefs of Staff authorised the creation of the Operational Groups on 23 December 1942. Recruiting for the Italian company began in April 1943. The men were mainly drawn from infantry and engineer companies, while wireless operators came from the Signals Corps and medical technicians from the Medical Corps. The men were chosen for their physical qualifications and linguistic abilities. The OSS SI branch provided assistance in the recruitment programme.

Since all the candidates came from the United States Army, it was assumed that they had completed basic training. OG instruction was specialised in nature, with emphasis on physical conditioning. Courses were designed to make the men proficient in demolition, small arms, scouting, patrolling and reconnaissance, first aid, unit security measures, living off the land, hand-to-hand combat, camouflage, map reading and compass use, and the equipment and methods of airborne and seaborne raids. Many of the tactical exercises were conducted at night. Operational training included mountain climbing, parachuting, amphibious operations, skiing, light artillery, radio operations and advanced espionage tactics. Aggressiveness of spirit and willingness to close with the enemy were stressed.

The Operational Group for Italy was the first to be activated as Company 'A' on 14 May 1943. Initially, the personnel sent overseas were all from Italian-American families, with origins in a variety of Italian regions where many different dialects were spoken. While most of those who joined them later in the field came from a similar background, it was not deemed essential. The first contingent consisted of seventeen officers and 126 enlisted men. Late in July, two officers and five enlisted men left by air for action in Italy. In August, the rest of the unit arrived at 'Station X', a tented camp in pine woods at El Biar, west of Algiers. Parachute training was only in its early stages when operations began.

One group went to Italian-occupied Corsica, together with a French force, to liberate the island in conjunction with the local *Maquis* and to harass the

German 90th Panzer Division, which was attempting to escape via the port of Bastia. The company suffered its first casualties on 24 September during an attack on a German convoy, losing an officer and two enlisted men. OG personnel also dropped into Sardinia (without a ground-reception party) to notify the Italian commanders of the terms of the Armistice and to pass on orders from their new government to cooperate with the Allies.

At first, the Americans were sceptical as to whether the partisan movement could develop in Italy as it had in the Balkans; however, they were soon made aware of the wish of the Italians to engage in armed resistance against the Nazi occupiers and their Fascist collaborators. In a report sent to the 1994 Venice conference, Max Corvo, former SI Operations Officer in Italy, related:

> The Italian Theatre of operations was unique in that an enemy country that was an absolute dictatorship should, mainstream in a global war, produce the kind of liberation movement that the CLNAI eventually gave the nation, winning the respect of the Allied leaders for its integrity, its sacrifice and its inspired leadership.

Over the course of four days at the end of September 1943, the people of Naples rose up. The Germans abandoned the city, leaving the port undamaged for the Allies to use.

On 13 October the Italian government declared war on Germany, being given the status of a co-belligerent. This offered the Allies the opportunity to recruit members of Italian Military Intelligence (SIM) as agents for the OSS and SOE and to obtain radio operators; these recruits were then trained in Allied procedures. At the same time, a number of young professionals and university students led by Raimondo Craveri offered their services to the Americans. The group became known as the Italian Resistance Organization (ORI), and its agents took part in OSS activities in the German-occupied north until the end of the war. Through its association with the central liberation committee in Milan, ORI played an important part in intelligence and policy decisions.

An OSS OG group joined the British SAS for Operation Simcol, which had the objective of rescuing escaped Allied prisoners of war who were at large in south-eastern Italy after the Armistice. Ten Americans were parachuted on 2 October, and another five were assigned to SAS units as interpreters and came in by sea. The commanding officer, Lieutenant Peter Sauro, and three enlisted men were captured in January 1944; they spent the rest of the war in German camps. The other agents remained behind the lines for up to nine months.

In the middle of October the company moved from 'Station X' to Ile Rousse, Corsica. The Operations Officer was Captain Albert Materazzi. He told me that they worked in close cooperation with the Balaclava Mission of SOE led by the Arctic explorer Captain Andrew Croft. OSS squads on American or

British patrol boats captured the islands of Capraia and Gorgona and set up outposts to observe enemy shipping, provide weather reports, and give early warning of aerial attacks on Corsica. Reconnaissance and sabotage of targets were also carried out on the island of Pianosa and on the Tuscan coast.

The OSS extended their activities with the partisans in January 1944, shortly before the landing at Anzio on the 22nd. Several bands operated in the bridgehead, and others were parachuted elsewhere in Latium. They attacked enemy units, sabotaged railway lines, destroyed fuel depots, and scattered triple-pointed nails on the roads.

Peter Tompkins was sent to Rome to set up the OSS operational base with a transmitter-receiver. Giuliano Vassali acted as his link with the Liberation Committee. The American recalled:

> Intercepted German signals and the Ultra deciphering at Bletchley Park in England went far toward assuring final victory, but little credit has been given to the vast amount of detailed intelligence collected and rapidly transmitted by partisan spies in Italy. Strategically, Ultra may have saved the day, but tactically its information was far slower in getting to where it was needed in the field than agent signals.
>
> During the crucial battles of Anzio in January and February 1944, for example, Ultra signals warning of Hitler's plans and of Field Marshal Albert Kesselring's attacks would arrive regularly at Allied headquarters at Caserta as many as three days after the attacks had already taken place. On the other hand, extremely accurate information gathered by the partisans, often directly from Kesselring's own headquarters, was sent via a secret OSS radio in Rome, on the air as many as five times a day, to be received simultaneously in Caserta and on the beachhead in time to repel these attacks.[1]

Company 'A' was designated First Contingent OG, 2677th Regiment OSS (Provisional), in May 1944. In August, the new commander of OSS in Italy, Colonel William Glavin, decided to merge all its units, using the new cover name of 'Company D, 2677th Regiment'. The headquarters was located at Siena, and later in Florence. The reorganisation made it possible for AFHQ and the 15th Army Group to closely monitor partisan operations throughout northern Italy and to coordinate actions in concert with regular forces. The Operational Groups were re-designated as the 2671st Special Reconnaissance Battalion Separate (Provisional). This eliminated the reference to OSS and better reflected the structure of an organisation with three companies and a headquarters unit.

Company 'A' moved to Siena on 1 September 1944 and was placed under the operational control of G-3 Special Operations of 15th Army Group, led by American Colonel John Riepe. The OSS Secret Intelligence branch was also involved, though their primary mission was to obtain strategic information.

They recruited agents from Italian military intelligence (SIM) and other disbanded units and infiltrated them into enemy territory by land, sea or air. The operatives often relied on partisans for support and reported to the Colonel in such cases. SOE also answered to him on the Fifth Army front, as did the SAS.

Close cooperation between the Americans and the Italians had already been established at an operational level when the prospects for unconventional warfare improved significantly after the liberation of Rome. Albert Materazzi related:

> During the Allied advance to the Gothic Line some excellent partisan groups were overrun and proved to be very useful in tactical situations. The bands in the north occupying the mountains were in a position to attack the German lines of communication. Obviously they had to be supplied and their operations coordinated with those of the regular army forces. This was the job for which the OGs were created.

The partisans were particularly active along the Gothic Line, the German defensive position that ran along the mountains from near Massa to just south of Rimini. OSS reports to the Allied General Staff during July and August 1944 revealed that the rebels intercepted half the German supplies. They caused 170 enemy casualties, destroyed ten railway bridges and many locomotives and wagons, and blew up railway lines in thirty-three places.

As the war escalated in the winter of 1944, the official log of Company A was full of various similar activities—new missions; supply drops to partisan organisations; unsuccessful atttempts due to weather conditions; reports of injuries; the loss of men killed in action; leave for men who had spent more than four months behind the lines; the aid given to downed airmen; radio contacts lost and re-established; men sent to the Mountain Warfare Training Centre; training in skiing and mountain climbing; more injuries in training and in action; money dropped to missions in sealed containers; money delivered to partisan commanders; a Bronze Star and a Silver Star awarded; heartwarming reports of praise for officers and enlisted men behind the lines; Purple Hearts for the wounded; a field commission to Second Lieutenant for an enlisted man; reinforcements sent to various missions; the crashing and burning of a plane, killing all on board; a B-24 flying in supplies shot down; a report that captured men were released from a prison camp; and more of the above.

Partisan Piero Boni took part in the Resistance in Rome and then led two OSS missions in Emilia. He told the 1994 Venice Conference:

> It is a well-known fact that the OSS established contacts with all political parties represented within the Italian Liberation Committee, avoiding political discrimination on the basis of predetermined decisions. This balanced attitude will not be easily forgotten by many an Italian partisan.

Personally I am convinced that this line of conduct lay fundamentally upon two basic convictions: first, a general trust in the Italian anti-Fascist forces, and, second, a will to conform to the principle of non-interference with the highly complicated political situation in Italy.

This, however, does not obviously imply that American forces in Italy did not follow their own established policy, nor that they lacked a legitimate position concerning the future of Italian politics, for one thing, they were certainly worried about the strength of the Communist component within the Resistance Movement. However, both the American Army and the OSS, with the pragmatic touch that distinguished them, were generally wise enough to maintain a distinction between the political and the military fronts.

General Donovan's policy was clear: 'In clandestine fighting, competence and courage count more than ideology.' The mutual trust was facilitated by the presence of large numbers of Italian-Americans in OSS forces. As a result, communication with the partisans was often both immediate and spontaneous, and this aided the success of joint military actions.

In early March 1945, Captain Materazzi asked the head of OG Peedee mission in Liguria, Captain Leslie Vanoncini, to provide an urgent report on the mainly Communist partisans of the Sixth Zone on behalf of Colonel John Riepe. On 15 January, Lieutenant-Colonel Richard Hewitt of No. 1 Special Force had written a long memorandum detailing the dangers of arming Communist divisions, supported by extracts of reports from various British missions. He recommended that only clothing, food and medicines be sent to them. Reports were also coming into Allied headquarters from the British Clover Mission, which worked alongside Peedee, but it was thought useful to also have a first-hand American account.

The Captain was tasked with describing the number and deployment of the partisans and also with assessing their political affiliations and intentions after the war. He found that the area command was organised and hierarchical:

> The partisan commanders of the zone have created an army which responds without exception to their commands—exactly as in our own army. Nothing is done by subordinate leaders of the divisions or brigades without the full consent of the zonal command.

In turn, the partisan leaders were completely loyal to their political leadership in the liberation committees and to the Allied military:

> Orders coming from Fifteenth Army Group, the CLN, and from Genoa are rules and not just guides for the command.... They have such control that political flare-ups are never heard of.

Above: From left to right: Joseph Stalin, Franklin D. Roosevelt, and Winston Churchill at the Tehran Conference, 28 November 1943. The inclusion of the Soviet Union as the third partner in the Grand Alliance with the United States and the United Kingdom had a profound effect on the course of the war, and on the Resistance movements in Italy and the rest of German-occupied Europe.

Below: Heavily-armed female Italian partisans. Out of 223,639 fighting partisans recognised officially in 1947, 35,000 were women. Many others acted as couriers or helped fugitive servicemen.

The United States 34th Infantry Division (the Red Bull) in fierce fighting on Monte Pantano, near Cassino, 29 November–3 December 1943. The line remained largely static over the winter.

General Mark Clark, Commander 5th Army, greeted by Monsignor Hugh O'Flaherty of the Rome Escape Organisation in Saint Peter's Square on 5 June 1944.

The British Type 3 Mark II clandestine radio, commonly known as the B2. The sets were issued to agents, resistance groups, and special forces operating in enemy territory.

Above: Soldiers of the United States 92nd Infantry Division operate a mortar near Massa, Tuscany, in November 1944. Allied missions embedded with the partisans in the Apennines ensured effective liaison with regular forces.

Below: Sherman tanks disembarking at Anzio from US LST 77 early in 1944. While Allied forces waited to break out of the bridgehead, intelligence collected by their agents and the partisans in Rome proved invaluable.

Italy-based B-24 Liberator bombers. The aircraft made many daring supply missions to the partisans, in addition to their combat role.

IN RICORDO DELL'EQUIPAGGIO DEL LIBERATOR KG 875 DEL 31° SQUADRON
SOUTH AFRICAN AIR FORCE CADUTO NEL VALLONE ARLENS
IL 12 OTTOBRE 1944 DURANTE UNA MISSIONE DI RIFORNIMENTO ALLE
FORZE DELLA RESISTENZA

CAPT. PILOT	BEUKES LEONARD von SOLMS	ANNI 26-S.A.A.F.
SGT. PILOT	ANSTEE GEORGE FREDERICK JESSE	ANNI 23-R.A.F.
LIEUT. NAVIGATOR	KRUGER MICHIEL COENRAAD FREDERICK DU PLODY	ANNI 29-S.A.A.F.
SGT. BOMB AIMER	FOSTER CHARLES LEA	ANNI 24-R.A.F.
SGT. W/O-A/G	WOODS HUBERT JOHN	ANNI 20-R.A.F.
LIEUT. A/G	SHIPMAN GAVIN D'ARCY	ANNI 27-S.A.A.F.
WARRANT OFF. A/G	FRANCIS DEREK AUBREY WESTON	ANNI 24-S.A.A.F.
SGT. W/O-A/G	PRYCE WILLIAM LESLIE	ANNI 20-R.A.F.

VALPRATO SOANA 27 LUGLIO 2013

Memorial at Valprato Soana, Piedmont, to the British and South African crew of Liberator KG 875, lost on the supply mission on 12 October 1944.

Flying Officer Thomas Roberts Millar, Royal Australian Air Force, missing in action on a supply mission to the partisans on 12 October 1944.

Left to right: former SOE agents Bill Pickering and Max Salvadori with ex-partisan Giuseppe Fulcheri at the unveiling of a plaque in memory of Captain John Keany at Cinaglio on 24 April 1988.

SOE Corporal 'Busty' Millard, radio operator on the sub-mission to the partisans of the Sixth Alpine Division (*Alpi*) led by Giovanni Toselli ('Otello').

Museum of the Resistance at Sperongia, Morfasso, in the Arda Valley, province of Piacenza.

The church at Mombarcaro, in the province of Cuneo, Piedmont, where the arms dropped with the Chariton Mission were hidden.

Weapons for the partisans—a British Bren light machine gun on an ammunition box, an Italian Beretta MAB submachine gun (top left), and a British Sten submachine gun (top right).

Uniforms for the partisans, as supplied by Allied parachute drops.

Victorious partisans enter Genoa in April 1945.

Soldiers of the Brazilian Expeditionary Force at Massarossa. The liberation of most of Tuscany in 1944 was made with tactical support provided by Allied missions and partisan forces.

Communist partisans in Florence, August 1944. The three in the front carry British Sten Guns.

The drop zone at Monesiglio, Piedmont, on 4 February 1945 for the SOE Chariton Mission to Major Enrico Mauri's autonomous partisans.

Partisans operating in the north of Italy, October 1944.

SWITZERLAND

GERMANY

FRANCE

Bolzano
OZAV

OZAK   Lubiana

Milano   Salò

Verona   Padova   Trieste

Torino   Venezia

Genova

Bologna

MONACO

Ligurian Sea   Firenze

SAN
MARINO

ITALIAN
SOCIAL
REPUBLIC

Adriatic Sea

FRANCE

KINGDOM
OF ITALY

Tyrrhenian Sea

Roma

KINGDO
OF ITAL

○○ Italian Social Republic (as of 1943)

○ German operational zones: OZAK (Operational Zone of the Adriatic Littoral) and OZAV (Operati
Zone of the Alpine Foothills)

A map of the Italian Social Republic (RSI) in the second half of 1943, with the liberated
Kingdom of Italy in the south and the two German Operational Zones in the north-east.

The Captain stated that the partisan leadership were responsible partners for the mission and ably carried out their functions of coordination and distribution of the weapons and supplies from the Allies. He also said that the political aspect of the entire region was of very little importance; the leaders of the zone were of more relevance:

> They have lived under Fascism all their lives and do not know how democracy works. They have heard little of how others are ruled. They know the wreck Fascism has made of Italy and all they want to do is free the country from this once powerful band ... I cannot see any danger of political flare ups, but it would be advisable to keep these young leaders occupied once the area is cleared.

However, in the mountains of Liguria the American Captain found that the most common sentiment was one of extreme anti-Fascism that transcended political affiliations. He wrote: 'I praise these men for what they have done, never considering the personal risk.'

On 26 February 1945 Field Marshal Albert Kesselring, the German Supreme Commander South-West, sent this message to army commanders and to the SS:

> Activities of the partisans in the western Apennines and along the Via Emilia, particularly in the area of Modena, Reggio and Parma, and south-west of them, as well as near Piacenza, have spread like lightning in the last ten days. The concentration of the partisan groups of varying political tendencies into one organisation, as ordered by the Allied High Command, is beginning to show clear results. The execution of partisan operations shows considerably more commanding leadership. Up to now it has been possible for us, with a few exceptions, to keep our vital rear lines of communication open by means of slight protective forces, but the situation threatens to change considerably for the worse in the immediate future. Speedy and radical counter measures must anticipate this development.
>
> It is clear to me that the only remedy, and the one which is unavoidably necessary to meet the situation, is the concentration of all available forces, even if this means temporary weakening in other places. I request you therefore to combine with 14th Army and the Army of Liguria in carrying out several large-scale operations which will nip in the bud the increasing activity of the partisans of northern Italy. Please let me have your proposals as to when these measures can be carried out and with what forces.

Company 'A' sent twenty-seven missions into enemy territory from September 1943 to May 1945. In addition, the responsibility for partisan bands at the front in tactical situations belonged to the OSS and its dedicated 5th and 8th Army detachments. As the Allied offensive stalled with the approach of winter 1944, the secret services ably coordinated the activities of the guerrilla forces in order to cause maximum discomfort to the enemy. As the result of a series of military and political agreements known as the Rome Protocols (see Chapter 3), signed by partisan and Allied leaders in December 1944, the missions embedded with the partisans were given an important coordinating role. They were to be consulted on all matters relating to armed resistance, anti-scorch and the maintenance of order.

During the final offensive, in the spring of 1945, there were ten OG missions in strategic areas of northern Italy—despite the bad weather and the limited availability of aircraft and supplies. The teams, totalling 120 men, helped train the partisans in the use of explosives and in commando tactics, and also provided weather reports and bomb assessments to the Air Force.

The Operational Groups also helped downed airmen evade capture by the enemy and return to Allied forces. The head of the Twelfth Air Force, Brigadier-General Charles T. Myers, sent a letter of commendation to the 2677th Regiment OSS on 13 June 1945. With reference to the Italian groups, he wrote:

> Company 'A' willingly assumed the extra burden of exfiltrating by land and sea, airmen of both 12th Air Force and Desert Air Force, even though it taxed them in accomplishment of their primary mission. Their complete cooperation in assisting airmen to evade capture by the enemy included direct instructions to their agents to render all possible aid: to help with money, food, clothing, hiding places and guides.

As the Fifth and Eighth armies broke through in the western and eastern sectors during the third week of April, the partisans went into action in a popular uprising coordinated by OSS and SOE officers in the field. Patriot forces took over Genoa, Turin and Milan. OSS assistant operations officer in SI Italy, Lieutenant Emilio Daddario, moved from Switzerland and captured the Fascist commander, Marshal Graziani, and Generals Bonomi and Sorrentino. Mussolini, meanwhile, had fallen into the hands of the partisans, and he was executed alongside his mistress and other leading Fascists on 28 April, despite American attempts to capture him.

After the German and Fascist surrender on 2 May, in some cases as many as two weeks elapsed before the arrival of Allied troops and the installation of military governors. In the interim, food and essentials for the civilian population were dropped to the OG teams. They worked with the partisans in administering the areas and helped to maintain order. Fascists and Germans suspected of being war criminals were rounded up and arrested.

These were the main Operational Group missions to enemy territory (in chronological order):

Bathtub 2 (Sardinia)
Fourth Group (Corsica)
Simcol (south-eastern Italy)
OP 2 (Capraia)
Polar 1 and 2 (Italian west coast)
OP 1 or Seneca (Gorgona)
Neptune (Leghorn)
Valentine (Genoa)
Chicago I (Pianosa)
Alpha (Anzio)
Chicago 2 (Pianosa)
Ginny I (Stazione Framura)
Balkis 1 and 2 (Pianosa)
Ginny 2 (Stazione Framura)
Walla Walla (Liguria)
Chrysler (near Como)
Ford (Val d'Aosta)
Aztec (near Belluno)
Cayuga (Parma)
Tacoma (near Cortina d'Ampezzo)
Peedee (Liguria)
Spokane or Sewanee (Valtellina)
Santee (Sondrio)
Roanoke (Oltrepo Pavese)
Choctaw (near Parma)

The OG operations with the partisans or in support of regular military forces drew unanimous praise from the Allied commanders. In May 1945, General Mark Clark sent a letter of commendation to the 2671st Special Reconnaissance Battalion. It read in part:

> The task of the men of this Company was a difficult one as they were constantly pursued and harassed by the enemy forces. With the knowledge that if captured, they probably would be tortured and executed by the enemy, these men volunteered for these extra hazardous missions. The outstanding success of partisan operations in the areas where these men operated, and the excellent intelligence as to enemy dispositions received, was in large measure due to the presence of these men and their leadership of partisan formations.

A letter of commendation from Colonel George L. King, head of the Special Operations Section, G-3 Allied Force Headquarters, included the paragraph:

> Operating continuously under the most difficult, nerve and body wracking conditions; by the very nature of the duties and missions assigned being always denied the just recognition which comes to the ordinary combat soldier in timely increments; faced with the ever present danger of ignominious extinction by a fanatically desperate enemy, you inaugurated, perfected and waged successfully for US forces a new and powerful type of warfare which we now know—from out of the mouth of the enemy himself—was the 'straw which broke the camel's back' of the Axis Forces in Italy, and helped bring the war here to a successful conclusion much earlier than had been anticipated.

The outstanding performance by the Operational Groups against the enemy from 15 April to 2 May 1945 was also honoured by a Presidential Distinguished Service Award on 18 July 1946. The story of the first Operational Group, and its successors in the same area, is the topic of the next chapter—from infiltration to liberation.

11

American Operational Groups in Liguria

The first United States OG mission to work with partisans in enemy territory was parachuted from three British aircraft at 1 a.m. on 12 August 1944. The planes were Halifaxes from No. 148 Squadron RAF—JP 254 D, piloted by Warrant Officer G. P. Bowser, EB 196 E, flown by Sergeant F. N. Snow, and JD 319 G, piloted by Flight Sergeant A. J. Toft. The aircraft had left Brindisi at 9 p.m.

The mission—codenamed 'Walla Walla'—arrived at a drop zone on Monte Aiona (1,692 metres), near Rezzoaglio in the Aveto Valley, Liguria. Their role was to operate with the partisans of the Sixth Zone and to provide liaison between them and Allied Armies Italy (AAI).

The mission was a section of fifteen uniformed men; it was led by Captain William Wheeler Jr, born in 1917, with Lieutenant Quayle Smith as second in command and wireless telegraphist. The enlisted men were all Italian Americans: Technical Sergeant Angelo Gallante; Corporals John Uccellini, Chester Scerra and Frederick Marchese; and Technicians Fifth Grade Joseph Alfieri, Thomas Cossuto, Cosmo Mangogna, Arthur Ruozzi, Arthur Roberta, Patric Scoleri, Hugo Collacicco, Charles Lotito and Ermenio DiSano.

The reception was organised by the OSS SI Locust team, which had infiltrated the area by sea, landing near Genoa, on 23 June. They were at the drop zone to welcome their compatriots. The partisan reception party was led by twenty-two-year-old Michele Campanella ('Gino'), leader of the *Severino* Battalion. He had been serving with Italian forces in Yugoslavia on the Armistice and managed to return to Italy. After only a few days at home in Genoa, Michele left for the mountains and joined the partisans. At the end of the winter he had been entrusted with organising the reception of airdrops. Two squads built huts and storehouses in three different mountain locations, camouflaging them with turf, but no supplies came—although Allied planes overflew the zone on several occasions.

The local partisans took their name from the hamlet of Cichero in the mountain commune of San Colombano Certenoli, only about 10 miles north of Chiavari. The group attracted traditional anti-Fascists, disbanded Italian soldiers and escaped prisoners of war. The band became famous for its military prowess and democratic ideals. Michele was appointed head of one of three detachments in March 1944. The partisans liberated neighbouring valleys and became known as the Third *Garibaldi* Brigade, but their expansion triggered enemy reprisals, and on 17 July the hamlet of Cichero was sacked and seven residents slain.

The partisans took up their positions on Monte Aiona on 12 August. They soon heard the sound of anti-aircraft fire from the coast and saw planes and parachutes overhead. A light north wind blew the parachutes away from the target and scattered men and supplies among the cliffs. The task of recovery was not completed until 8 a.m. Some of the parachutists sustained minor injuries due to the rough terrain, and they were carried away on rudimentary stretchers prepared on the spot.

The mission was welcomed with open arms. Once introductions had been made, William ordered that chocolate, whisky and cigarettes should be distributed among the partisans. Apart from those posted for guard duty, the rebels gathered around the storehouses for the Americans to instruct them on the use of plastic explosives, mortars and a bazooka, and how to distribute several sacks of propaganda material.

Lieutenant Smith and three other soldiers remained on the mountain to set up a wireless telegraphy reception and to provide further training to the partisans. The group was also to monitor enemy troop movements from information provided by the rebels' own intelligence sources.

After a frugal meal consisting of mashed, roast chestnuts, the injured soldiers and the supplies were loaded onto sixty mules. The group was escorted off the mountain by a detachment of thirty partisans. Once they reached the roadway between Villanoce and Rezzoaglio, the muleteers were dismissed, and half the partisans returned to Monte Aiona. The others led the Americans to a bus, which took them to Gorreto; here, they were introduced to the commanders of the Sixth Partisan Zone. The vehicle was followed by trucks loaded with supplies from the airdrop.

William was pleasantly surprised. In his end-of-mission report he wrote:

At the time the mission was introduced into northern Italy little was known of partisan activity there. The briefing was confined to the broad instruction of contacting a partisan group and harassing the enemy. The impression created led us to believe that the mission would be strictly operational, coordinating efforts with a small band of partisans, living in the mountains and making raids upon targets as they presented themselves. This conception was proved a delusion when upon arrival a modern passenger bus transported the group over nearly 20 miles of road to a headquarters building. This was in 'liberated Italy' from where the Nazi-Fascists had been driven, allowing peaceful occupation of the region.

The partisans were in a position to harass the enemy lines of communication, but they were also in desperate need of supplies and training. William recalled that until the arrival of the mission, shortages were affecting military operations: 'It was the partisans' theory that available material should be kept for defensive actions against the enemy in the mop-up routine.' Between 12 and 25 August, a large quantity of supplies arrived through airdrops to Monte Aiona and to a nearby target at Cappella delle Lame (1,543 metres). The airlift had to be suspended when the enemy launched a roundup on 26 August, which lasted ten days. The Americans and the partisan command established a temporary headquarters across the regional border at Selva di Ferriere, in the province of Piacenza.

Despite the crisis, the partisans asked the mission to refrain from launching a counter-attack. William recalled:

> The mission was regarded by the partisan commanders as their saviours. We were to supply them adequately, obtain air support and be their advisors. In so far as being operational, their contention was that they had men to do the work. We were to devote our abilities to supply, instruction and liaison.

Meanwhile, the partisan organiser of the airdrops, Michele Campanella, had led his men into the hills above Genoa. The *Severino* Battalion operated on the outskirts of the city until the liberation. Michele remained in contact with the mission to provide intelligence and to receive guidance on enemy targets. He also established close liaison with the successor OSS operational group, codenamed 'Peedee', which was parachuted to Monte Antola on 18 January 1945 under Captain Leslie Vanoncini. British SOE mission Clover, commanded by Lieutenant-Colonel Peter McMullen, was dropped at the same time.

After several weeks of working with various partisan groups, William concluded that they should be unified and that uncooperative units should not be supplied. He arranged a general conference that included all division and brigade commanders of the area and representatives of the Committee for National Liberation. As a result of American help, the rebels were able to carry out a significant number of actions against the enemy. William reported:

> Aside from military considerations, the presence of an American mission served as a constant reminder of the Allies' desire to aid the partisan cause and also as a signifier of the unification of efforts against a common enemy.

During the period Walla Walla was in the field, they arranged for over 100 tons of military and non-combat supplies to be delivered to partisans across various drop zones. The materials were distributed on the basis of agreements with the partisan command and on William's judgement on the fighting prowess of the formations. An airdrop was made to the Justice and Liberty Brigade of Fausto Cossu at Pecorara, in the Tidone Valley of Piacenza, on 12 November; they refused to share the contents of the containers with the partisans of the Sixth Zone, so William suspended their access to further supplies.

The mission was in daily contact with OG headquarters, providing tactical information on enemy dispositions and movements and identifying possible bombing targets. The team guided the partisans in operations scheduled by the OG HQ and AAI. The mission also established links with Major Gordon Lett, British Liaison Officer in the Fourth Partisan Zone, whose forces provided an escape line for downed airmen, prisoners of war, agents and couriers.

As the various partisan units received supplies and training and the frequency of their military attacks increased, the inevitable enemy response forced the regional partisan headquarters to move frequently. Finally, on 12 December, the Germans launched an offensive across the entire Sixth Partisan Zone. The partisans resisted for three days before being forced to disperse. The mission reported that the rebels were taking advantage of their deployment in the mountains, hiding their weapons and going to ground until the offensive ceased. The section was ordered to return to Allied territory. The men had been in the field for nineteen weeks. Albert Materazzi, the Operations Officer of the Operational Groups, told me:

> There is no doubt that Walla Walla was a success. Colonel Riepe was not happy that they came out early and I was ordered to replace the mission immediately with Peedee. This time I did not make the mistake of sending in an entire section, which Wheeler soon found out that he did not need and was a burden. The partisans did not need more men, many of them were from the Italian Army, including officers. What they needed was communication with Allied headquarters, arms and ammunition, winter clothes, boots, medical supplies, and specialized personnel to teach demolitions and our new arms such as the bazooka. After Walla Walla, I only sent in a few missions as they were needed. I am sure that Wheeler would not have come out if he did not feel that they had become a burden to the partisans, using food and ammunition they badly needed. Also, the partisans felt a need to help protect them.[1]

The Walla Walla team left for Allied territory on 21 December, escorted by partisan guides. They marched across the mountains and reached the Rossano Valley in northern Tuscany. Their arrival was recorded in the book *Rossano* by Major Gordon Lett, another escaper from PG 29 Veano on the Armistice. He set up an International Battalion of partisans and was appointed as Liaison Officer by SOE. The Major was awarded the British DSO and the Italian Silver Medal for Military Valour. He recalled his meeting with Captain Wheeler:

> The stranger stooped as he came through the door, and then stood still, accustoming his eyes to the gloom and smoke. Then:
> 'Is Major Lett here?' he said.
> I was relieved at the friendly American accent, and stood up.
> 'What can I do for you?'
> The stranger smiled.
> 'You've got darned good security,' he said. 'I and my men have been wandering round this God-darned valley for hours, and nobody would tell us where you were. He dropped on to the bench. 'My name is Wheeler. We've come from the 6th Zone.'[2]

William produced a crumpled envelope containing a short message from the Special Force colonel heading the British mission in the Genoa area. It requested that assistance be given to the Americans to travel through the lines. The other members of the mission entered one by one, and they were soon joined in the room by curious villagers. Major Lett recalled that the soldiers 'were well armed, and equipped with American uniforms, and this gave a sense of security to the onlookers that they had not experienced for many years past'. That night, the Americans slept on the floor of the room while the villagers kept guard outside.

In the morning, Major Lett collected a small party of guides to take the mission on their way. He also provided them with a letter to Lieutenant Daniele Bucchioni in the Calice Valley; it asked him to escort them across the marble mountains of Carrara and through the Gothic Line to Allied Forces.

The Major's radio had broken down a week earlier, and the American operator was able to contact headquarters on his behalf. The telegraphist reported that there was a special message and that an immediate reply was required; this was the proposal to send in British troops to the Rossano Valley, and it was eagerly accepted. The Second Battalion, SAS, arrived on 27 December in Operation Galia. The Americans had reached the United States 92nd Infantry Division at Azzano the day before.

The partisan leader who had first greeted the mission on Monte Aiona in August, Michele Campanella, was wounded three times in action. On the liberation, he commanded the partisan police in Genoa. When the force was dissolved, Michele served in the Corps of Public Security and reached the rank of Lieutenant-General. He was awarded the Italian Silver Medal for Military Valour and the American Bronze Star. The citation for the United States honour reads:

Commandant of the *Severino* Battalion, for heroic acts relative to military operations against the enemy during the period of 1 and 2 May 1945: As commandant of the *Severino* Brigade of the Italian partisan movement, Michele Campanella, despite the lack of weapons and equipment, continually caused trouble to the enemy, carrying out acts of sabotage and attacks against convoys and troops. He demonstrated ingenuity and great skill and with unswerving loyalty and heroism brought to fruition the plans of the Allied Command, making use of the forces and materials at his disposal to the great benefit of the Allied forces. The commendable contribution of Michele Campanella and his organization to the cause of his country and to that of the Allies is worthy of the highest traditions of the people who love freedom.

On 18 January 1945 Captain Vanoncini and five men parachuted into Liguria in the new Peedee OG mission. They were followed on 21 March by two more agents. On 5 April, the second in command, Lieutenant Vincent Bartolomeo, and eight other men were also dropped, making up the mission to section strength, ready for the final offensive. With two exceptions, the same team had taken part in OG Mission Helen to southern France in the summer of 1944.

Living conditions were poor during January and February. The weather was very cold, and the snow was 3 feet deep. There were constant enemy attacks. The men slept on straw, and two of them contracted scabies; however, the mission was able to purchase medicine to treat the sick men when the partisans liberated the town of Ottone at the end of February.

The drop zone on 5 April was rather small, and the aircraft was forced to make three passes, dropping three men each time. Medical Technician Third Grade Philip Francis was in the second group. He was the son of a farmer and coalminer; he came from a family of Italian immigrants named 'Francesconi', who lived in a rural area of Pittsburg. His skills were called upon immediately when one of his colleagues hit a tree in the descent. Philip grabbed a canteen from one of the partisans sent to welcome them, raised his friend's head, and told him to have a drink of water. The soldier suddenly jumped up and shouted, 'You son of a bitch! You're trying to poison me.' Philip raised the canteen to his lips and realised that it was not water but *grappa*, 'the honour drink of all good Italian partisans, the medicine that cures all ills'.

For the next three or four nights the group was housed in a small village called Pietranera, in the commune of Rovegno. The Americans trained the partisans in the use of mortars and machine guns, but most of their time was spent organising the reception of supplies at eighteen different locations. Three or four men were sent to each target along with about ten partisans. The materials included weapons and ammunition, explosives, motorcycles, petrol, clothing, food, paper for printing, propaganda material and medical supplies. In total, 115 aircraft supplied the Peedee Mission.

The objective of the OG was to cooperate with the British SOE Clover Mission and the 7,000 partisans located in the Sixth Zone in order to prevent the Axis troops retreating to Germany. The goal was to force as many of them as possible to surrender and to confiscate their weapons. The mission was also to provide military instruction and combat training to the partisans. The SOE responsibility was mainly to provide intelligence to the advancing Allied forces.

Philip told the 1994 Venice Conference of OSS veterans and former partisans:

Cooperation between the two groups was fair, with all decisions of importance passed to each other. The British did keep mostly to themselves. I can remember seeing Colonel McMullen once and Major Davidson twice.

The partisans were professional, kind and friendly:

Commander Miro fought in France, Yugoslavia and Spain. He far exceeded other commanders in military leadership and also claimed no political affiliation. Vice Commander Bisagno, twenty-five years old, wanted a free Italy … The man called Americano was a great combat fighter … Commissar Ugo kept the books for Zone Six and acted as the chaplain for the group. Medicine was Vuccio's only interest. Tigre was a young man blessed with a vibrant personality. These great men are but a few of the thousands of partisans who deserve our thanks.

The partisan who influenced Philip most was known as 'Doctor Dolo'— real name Leopold Rumberg—a Russian graduate of the American Medical School in Ankara, Turkey. Philip was surprised to find that his own expertise in combat medicine was not called upon, but he thought that part of the reason could have been that security was very good from mid-April, and this made penetration by the Germans and Fascists difficult. However, it was with Doctor Dolo that he saw the great medical and dental care that was available in the Sixth Zone. Another partisan doctor—under the alias of 'Vuccio'— organised hospitals and first aid stations by converting rooms of farmhouses and recruiting a dozen medics and even more civilian helpers.

On 12 April, Philip and Doctor Dolo reached the small town of Varzi, headquarters of the OG Mission Roanoke (led by Captain Rawleigh Taylor). The mission's medic was Leo Francis, Philip's twin brother. The Americans heard that President Roosevelt had died, and they supposed correctly that the former Vice President, Harry S. Truman, had become the new President and Commander in Chief.

Within a few days the partisans started the drive to liberate Genoa. They freed fellow rebels and prisoners of war from various dungeons as the enemy fled northwards. The released men were provided with clothing, shoes, confectionery, and cigarettes, and they were given medical care. The city was liberated on 27 April, and the last captives were released from the notorious *Casa dello Studente* SS headquarters. The partisans set up a prison in the basement of the Hotel Verdi for high-ranking Germans and Fascists. For some of the rebels this was a time to settle old scores, but even though members of another OG Mission (codenamed 'Ginny 2') had been summarily executed by the Germans, Captain Vanoncini forbade his men from going anywhere near a torture chamber or seeking revenge.

Meanwhile, a third OG mission was also experiencing the culmination of its work with the partisans in the south of the sector. After a delay of nearly two months, on 8 March Lieutenant Rawleigh Taylor had parachuted alone to the drop zone at Pietranera to lead the Roanoke Operational Group. The mission was to liaise with partisans west of the Scrivia Valley in order to instruct and assist them, to coordinate operations, and to lay on air supply drops. After establishing a safe base for operations, the mission would embark on its primary role of guerrilla raids and ambushes against enemy units and installations. The team were also to transmit intelligence to headquarters and cooperate with any other Allied missions in the area.

The main partisan units with which the Roanoke mission operated were the *Aliotta* Division (commanded by Domenico Mezzadra—battle name 'Americano'), with a total of 600 men, the *Capettini* Brigade (led by Angelo Ansaldi), the *Gramsci* Division of 500 men, and the *Masia* Division, with 400 men.

Rawleigh recalled that the morale of the partisans always seemed high, partly due to increased discipline, wearing of uniforms, supply drops of all types of equipment, and the presence of Allied missions. He described 'Americano' as one of the finest commanders he ever encountered. The partisan was born in the United States in 1920 at Windsor Locks, Connecticut. The family returned to the commune of Broni, in the province of Pavia, in 1933. The young man experienced the highs and lows of partisan life for a year before being appointed leader of all the partisans in the Oltrepo Pavese region in February 1945—a role he held until 9 April.

In late March, Italo Pietra ('Edoardo') became Vice Commander of the Sixth Zone under Antonio Ukmar ('Miro'), superseding Americano. Edoardo, a veteran of the Italian wars in Ethiopia and Albania and a member of military intelligence (SIM), had played a prominent part in the *Garibaldi* brigades since the Armistice. The mission arranged supplies for all the forces under his control—at first only the *Aliotta* Division, but later also the *Gramsci* and *Masia* divisions in the *Oltrepo Pavese* grouping.

Five more men arrived for the mission on 21 March, as well as another two for Captain Vanoncini's Peedee mission. Rawleigh set up an operational headquarters at Brallo and established a drop zone nearby, which was codenamed 'Lynn'. On 1 April he was accidentally shot in the left hand with a pistol; two other Americans were also slightly injured. The Lieutenant's wound required bed-rest until 9 April, the day that the final eight men for the Roanoke mission were parachuted. With the full section now in the field, a new base was created in a farmhouse at Pietragavina, 5 miles north of Varzi and about 20 miles south of Pavia.

The mission concentrated on the distribution of weapons, ammunition and clothing for the partisans as further supply drops were made. Training sessions were held on the use of mortars and bazookas. Other members of the mission left to reconnoitre Route 45, between Bobbio and Ottone, and Route 10, south of Voghera, in two- and three-man teams.

On some of the operations they were joined by Able Seaman James Wilde, an escaped British prisoner of war. He had been captured in April 1943 when the submarine HMS *Sahib* was scuttled after being attacked by Italian ships and aircraft. James was sent to a villa near Arezzo for interrogation and then, mysteriously, to a camp near Hamburg, Germany. In July he was similarly inexplicably returned to Italy and camp 52 Chiavari. James managed to jump from a cattle truck on the train taking the prisoners to Germany after the Armistice, and he received aid and shelter from the people of Voghera. When his first helper was denounced and arrested, he gave himself up to the Blackshirts; however, he again managed to escape. He became a noted partisan leader, earning the award of the British Empire Medal for the 'organisation of partisan activities'.

Rawleigh met Captain Vanoncini at Brallo on 18 April to discuss further plans. The next day, the Lieutenant visited several partisan formations with Edoardo and found that the men looked very fit, but also that they lacked weapons and ammunition due to expansion in numbers. Two days later, the mission received an order to attack Tortona, but the target was changed to Voghera overnight. The following day, Rawleigh met with Americano and Edoardo and they discussed plans for the offensive. It was decided that the mission would accompany the *Aliotta* Division up Route 10.

The attack began with a drive on Rivanazzano on 25 April. After prolonged negotiations at a German outpost, a colonel, five officers and 200 soldiers reluctantly surrendered to the Lieutenant. The partisans began to move on Voghera that night. There were only a few Fascists left in the town, and they were cleared by early morning. A German column of twelve trucks and 150 men also surrendered on the outskirts.

Early on 27 April, an excited partisan told Rawleigh that a force of about 1,000 Germans was preparing to march on Voghera from the south. Defences were immediately put up outside the town, but the attack failed to materialise. Sergeant Frederick Orbach rode a bicycle under a white flag to speak to the German officers. Early that night, their commander voluntarily surrendered his troops and thirty-five horses. Voghera was completely under partisan control by morning. The mission also accompanied the rebels in the occupation of several towns before the arrival of Allied forces—Godiasco, Rivanazzano, Casteggio, Stradella, Castel San Giovani, Casei Gerola and Broni.

Three men were sent north to Piacenza, where they successfully made contact with the advancing United States Thirty-Fourth Infantry Division. On 30 April the mission moved to Tortona and met a reconnaissance group of the Ninety-Second Division. A lieutenant accompanied the agents back to Voghera, and all the prisoners of the section were turned over to his control. Rawleigh was promoted to Captain and withdrawn for hospital treatment of his wounded hand. The rest of the mission left Voghera in three captured vehicles to return to base on 15 May. The Special Reconnaissance Battalion was dissolved on 19 June 1945.

12

The Liberation of Genoa

On 18 January 1945, British SOE Clover Mission (also known as 'M 12') made a perfect daylight landing on the south-eastern slopes of the highest peak in northern Liguria, Monte Antola (1,597 metres), north-east of Genoa. The drop zone (DZ) was controlled by the Americans, and the six-man OSS OG Peedee team, commanded by Captain Leslie Vanoncini, parachuted in at the same time.

The Special Force mission was the main one for Liguria in addition to part of Lombardy south of the River Po (known as the 'Oltrepo Pavese') and the province of Piacenza in Emilia. Eventually there were also four secondary missions; one was in Imperia, led by Captain Robert Bentley; one in Savona, led by Major Vivian Johnston, after the capture of five other agents; one in Voghera, led by Captain Basil Irwin; and one in Piacenza, led by Major Stephen Hastings. Another mission was already established in northern Tuscany under former prisoner of war Major Gordon Lett, and it had strong links with the province of Spezia in Liguria.

The British Liaison Officer was Lieutenant-Colonel Peter McMullen, whose family has run the firm of McMullen and Sons, Hertfordshire brewers, since 1827. In his official report, he wrote:

> I was lucky enough to have as my second in command Major (now Lieutenant-Colonel) Basil Davidson, with whom I had worked previously. He not only spoke fluent Italian and German, but also had considerable knowledge of Italian affairs.[1]

The Major was already an accomplished journalist, having worked on *The Economist* and the *Evening Star* (among other publications) before being recruited to the Army in December 1939. His many books include *Special Operations Europe*, published in 1980, which includes both a colourful account of the mission and a commentary on the differing beliefs and intentions of the partisans and the Allies.

In his 1994 autobiography *The Drums of Memory*, the former BLO for the mission to Piacenza, Sir Stephen Hastings, wrote that Colonel McMullen had a real knowledge of the oddities and limitations of guerrilla war, and that he was under no illusions:

> Peter came of a conventional, conservative, county family and his political views were entirely consistent. Basil was an intellectual and a Marxist— albeit a romantic one. This would not have mattered except for the fact that all partisan life is governed by politics and the mountains were full of well-organised Communist bands. It was much to the credit of Peter and Basil that their political disagreements were never bitter and their mission an unqualified success.[2]

Completing the Clover team were an Italian officer, Lieutenant Wochiecevich ('Elio'), and Corporal (later Sergeant) George Armstrong, the radio operator, who had served in the same capacity on the Major's last mission in Yugoslavia.

Basil recalled their arrival in Liguria:

> The journey was short and comfortable. No long distance dropping at night any more, but a leisurely start after breakfast from an airstrip near Leghorn. No hours of crouching in a stone-cold fuselage, but twenty minutes' pleasant flying up the coast beside the shining blue Tyrrhenian, 1,500 metres below, before turning inland with an umbrella of four British Spitfires larking overhead. And then across peaks and folds of frozen mountains, climbing from the Riviera, until the pilot found his signals on the ground and slowed and fell to 170 metres or so. And at last a leap and sunlit drop to a land of lovely snow. A group of partisans was waiting in the snow.[3]

Two of the men introduced themselves as Miro and Marzo. Basil recalled that neither had any marks of rank—nor even uniforms, apart from a red scarf— but that both were armed. They were in their forties. Miro, the younger, was Antonio Ukmar from Trieste. A railwayman by occupation, he left Italy in the 1920s under Fascist pressure, went to the Soviet Union, and later fought as a guerrilla in Spain, Ethiopia and France. In the summer of 1944, 'Miro' had arrived in Genoa and become zone commander in the mountains. Marzo was Giovanni Battista Canepa, a journalist from nearby Chiavari. He had been imprisoned by the Fascists many times, and he had also fought with the *Garibaldi* Brigades in Spain. Following the 1943 Armistice, 'Marzo' helped form one of the first armed groups—the famous band of *Cichero*, which took its name from a little hamlet in the mountains.

The British mission was taken along snowbound tracks to a huddle of cottages perched on the upper slopes of Monte Antola at Capanne di Carrega. The partisans had made their headquarters in the inn, which was half-cottage, half-refuge. The SOE men stayed three days. In his official report, Peter recalled:

> The partisans' welcome was very cordial, and we had the impression that they were more than a little surprised to receive such an apparently imposing mission after what had seemed to them to be long months of neglect on our part.

The special operations team had a dual role—liaising between the partisan formations and 15th Army Group and between the new civil administration and the Allied Military Government when the enemy withdrew.

The directives for phase one were:

1. The primary target should be intelligence of enemy order of battle, movements, intentions, minefields, etc.
2. Partisan formations should be encouraged to carry out sharp, stinging attacks on enemy columns, command posts, etc., without risking their hand in large-scale operations, which, it was argued, would only result in their rapid elimination as a fighting force.
3. Partisans should in every case prepare themselves for an all-out effort in conjunction with an eventual Allied offensive, the signal for which would be given by the Army Group Commander.

In his summary, Peter related the practical problems of working with other Allied secret agencies in the same area:

> It had been impossible to arrive at any agreement for distribution of work or spheres of influence between No. 1 Special Force and OSS, and both organisations (OSS in three distinct and uncoordinated parts—SI, SO and OG) were working independently in the field and at rear headquarters. To anyone with experience of field conditions this spelt the most dire confusion.

As a result, he was obliged to make a private agreement with his OSS colleague, Captain Vanoncini. The Americans would look after supplies and training, while the British were to concentrate on intelligence in all its aspects, tactical planning, liaison with the CLN and the regional command, and political aspects generally.

Peter noted that support from the partisans appeared a remote prospect in January 1945:

During late November and the whole of December the enemy had driven with considerable forces throughout the whole great quadrilateral formed by the seacoast, Route 62, Routes 9 and 10 and Route 35. Many partisan formations had suffered so badly as to have gone virtually out of business altogether, some for the time being, but others, it appeared, for the duration. The enemy had used a large part of the 162nd Turkestan Division and considerable Republican and Fascist forces, and had used them, learning by experience, in multiple columns converging on prearranged points over a period of weeks, and often also doubling back on their tracks.

Whatever liaison there had been between the provinces of Piacenza and Genoa had ceased to exist, and the difficulty was further increased by the arrival through the lines of the only American team (Walla Walla) active in that area. We therefore landed with a large question mark before us.

The mission learned that the partisan force numbered between 2,000 and 2,500 men. There were four main formations; the largest was the *Cichero* Division, which operated east of the Scrivia Valley and along the coast. Six brigades had suffered badly. The others were more or less intact, but they were tired and somewhat dispirited. The *Americano* Division was deployed along the Bobbio to Voghera road in the Oltrepo Pavese area. It was doubtful if it numbered 500 men, and most of its equipment had been lost to the enemy. The *Mingo* Division, with three brigades in the west, was also greatly weakened and scarcely in a position to fight anyone. Finally, there was a unit of about 200 men called the 'Mobile Brigade *Caio*', which was centred on Santo Stefano d'Aveto. It had moved with its commander, naval officer Ernesto Poldrugo ('Istriano'), from the province of Piacenza after disagreements with the *Stella Rossa* partisan formation in the Nure Valley.

Peter recalled that on the whole they found remarkably little political trouble:

> Nine tenths of the formations of the Sixth Zone were *Garibaldini* and the remainder mainly *Giustizia e Libertà*—Action Party. The zone command and the commands of the *Garibaldi* brigades were predominantly Communist, however it must be clearly said that this does not mean that the leaders were all Communists or that the rank and file were mostly Communist. The leading personalities on the zone command were undoubtedly Communists of conviction and of long experience, by no means crude hotheads, who understood their absolute need for collaboration with the Allies and with non-Communist elements among Italians themselves. Their strength lay precisely in their own wealth of political experience, their high standard of discipline and political understanding, and the support of their party, which was very highly organised in Genoa.

Basil related that they had dropped in the wake of one major enemy sweep across the mountains, and, as they soon found, on the eve of another. He added:

> Troops under German officers now aimed not so much at destroying partisan units, which they found difficult, as at robbing the partisans of village support by terrorising the villagers, which they found easy.

In his summary, Peter wrote:

> The enemy's flagging interest was apparently whipped up to new efforts by the exaggerated stories he received of waves of Allied parachutists landing in the mountains. He came after us and following one or two undignified withdrawals we kept moving at almost daily intervals for two or three weeks. But given the excessively broken nature of the ground we were usually at least one jump ahead of the nearest column and this enabled us to keep open our contact with base and to send a large volume of traffic.
>
> The general position in the area occupied by *Cichero*, into which we had dropped and in which for various reasons we decided to make our headquarters, was bad. Enemy drives had been very successful in disrupting the internal organisation, confidence and morale of all these formations. The season was winter, and a cold winter with deep snow at that. There was little or no prospect of the long expected Allied offensive, and perhaps most important of all, the partisans had no Allied liaison mission. They could therefore hope for little or no supplies and for no recognition.

After the enemy roundup of December 1944, which had forced the OSS Walla Walla mission to cross the lines, the zonal command had been forced to revert to basic guerrilla warfare rather than attempting to hold an occupied area in the mountains around Monte Antola. However, the leaders were not at all demoralised and had already anticipated the Army Group directive to cut formations to their minimum size by sending home all those who had weakened during the recent drive. The arrival of Allied missions—with the promise of recognition and supplies they held—put fresh heart into the partisans:

> The presence of the missions meant that it would be worthwhile, perhaps even necessary, to hold the enemy out of a certain chosen area in a more or less permanent way. The partisans fixed on the complex of mountain ridges linked with the passes at Capanne di Caregga and Capanne di Pei. Heavy snowstorms sealed this decision by making movement almost impossible. The tide was turned by a famous action in the upper Val Borbera on 30 January when a German column of thirty-two men was captured intact, with one officer and all their equipment. The *rastrellamento* continued with varying fortunes until

the middle of February, but morale was already rising and this success was followed rapidly by others of the same magnitude. By the end of February, the number of German prisoners held was a problem in itself.

Another factor making for improved morale was the slowly awakened sympathy of the peasants. The men in the formations were almost all from the towns, mainly Genoa. They had little knowledge of, or interest in, peasant ways and the peasants responded by resenting their intrusion and the additional dangers it meant for them. This lack of sympathy was occasionally acute. On the whole it seems to have decreased as the spring approached and in the end there was even cordiality.

Basil recalled that couriers from Miro found them by the middle of February, and they passed on the news that his units had launched a counter-offensive:

Reaching him again, we learned that there had been plenty of hard fighting around Antola, up the valleys leading from the plains and from Genoa. We had seen nothing of that, but at least we had learned the terrain. We were beginning to feel at home in these mountains.[4]

Peter set out how their actions were prioritised:

We decided that in view of the time factor it would be best to concentrate on the areas of greater tactical importance to the east of the Scrivia Valley and on the problem of Genoa itself. We had been able to forward several couriers via Major Lett (and later Major Henderson) through the lines and our W/T link remained extremely good.

The formations to the east of the Scrivia were by this time receiving ample, and perhaps more than ample, supplies of all kinds of equipment dropped by parachute. Their morale had vastly improved. The worst of the winter had passed and the enemy had showed decided signs of having had enough of it. It was agreed with the Zone Command, therefore, to push their units closer down to their main targets—the lines of communication and prisoner-taking points—and we decided to reinforce our missions. Major Johnston, Captain Brown and Flight Lieutenant Rippingale accordingly arrived with necessary W/T operators and equipment on 21 March. [The Major headed the secondary mission to Savona and the other officers formed another satellite mission in Piacenza, which was code-named Insulin. See Chapter 15].

The enemy deployed the whole of 135 Fortress Brigade on anti-partisan duties, reinforced by large numbers of navy personnel who had gone through short infantry and anti-tank training courses. There were also two battalions of *Bersaglieri*—one to the east of Genoa and one to the west—and part of

162 Division available for *rastrellamenti*, as well as local Black Brigades and Republican troops drawn from the provincial depots at Genoa, Alessandria and Piacenza.

However, this was unequal to a large-scale drive. All the Germans and Fascists could do was to perpetuate their attempts to contain the partisan formations by a series of more-or-less unrelated strikes. This caused the enemy to suffer around 3,000 casualties in the area east of the Scrivia Valley. The mission interrogated more than 200 German soldiers, gaining a fairly complete picture of their order of battle. The changing balance produced a position in which by 5 April, when the Army Commander ordered the all-out effort for formations east of Route 45, the rebels had occupied and freed practically the whole central mountain area east of the Scrivia. They were ranging as far as Route 62, where formations of other zones were active.

Various partisan units cleared the enemy out of their remaining advanced points. The *Coduri* Brigade was active on Route 1, and they actually occupied Sestri Levante for some hours. Formations in the *Cichero* area had moved right down into the Scrivia Valley and were harassing the enemy on both sides of the main roads. In the Oltrepo Pavese, the formations commanded now by 'Edoardo', with Captain Basil Irwin as liaison, were also busy on the Via Emilia (Route 10) and down to the Po itself. Morale was high.

The main mission of four eventually grew to sixteen, made up of five British officers, four 'other ranks', three ex-prisoners of war, and four Italian officers. On 14 April, Captain Gordon, Lieutenant Richards, Royal Navy Volunteer Reserve, and two wireless telegraphy (W/T) operators arrived by parachute. A few days later, they were joined by Captain Murphy, Royal Army Medical Corps, who had walked up from the Spezia area, via the Piacentino, having collected some very useful medical intelligence on the way. Captain Gordon and one W/T operator were sent to join *Coduri* Brigade and report on the position in the Chiavari area, and Gordon was able to send valuable information on the progress of the battle. An Italian officer, Lieutenant Quattrocolo (Aldo), was also dropped at this time for courier duties; the mission formed a very good impression of his abilities and sense of duty.

As the prospect of liberation came ever closer, the part the Resistance would play became the main topic of discussion. On 10 April the Communist Party issued its famous Directive 16, which led directly to the signing of the order for the national uprising by all five parties in the CLNAI. The main points of the directive read:

1. Partisan formations will attack and eliminate Nazi-Fascist headquarters and effect the liberation of cities, towns and villages ... the appropriate organisations will proclaim a general strike...
2. The enemy will be faced with the following alternatives: 'Surrender or die.'

3. On no account whatsoever must our comrades in military or civil
organisations accept any proposal or advice or consider any plan designed
to limit, prevent or obstruct the national uprising. A combination of
firmness, tact and skill must be employed in all discussions with Allied
military missions which have elected to be the mouthpiece for those who
favour a wait and see attitude and are therefore inclined to attach too
little importance to our urgent requests for the arms and ammunition
needed to ensure the success of the insurrection. In the circumstances, we
must be prepared to face the fact that the Allies may decide for one reason
or another to withhold their support, instead of making the contribution
for which we have asked.

The Ligurian Liberation Committee had finalised its own 'Plan A' for
insurrection about a week earlier. It provided for a full-scale assault on enemy
positions in all the towns of the Riviera, and especially Genoa. The plan
brought the Resistance directly into conflict with the intentions of the Allies.

The partisan military command in the region had provided its commanders
with guidance on relations with Allied missions. On 25 March, the CVL
stated that their General Command in Milan had stressed that it was essential
for them to ensure the personal safety of the members of the missions, the
delegates of the Allied Command on which the CVL depended, and ordered
them to collaborate as closely as possible. However, the guidance also
mentioned the necessity to uphold the spirit of national dignity, and that some
formations had behaved in a way that was incompatible with this principle:

> Certain partisan commands have failed to realise that the function of the
> Allied missions, which act as liaison organisations between us and the Allied
> Command, is purely the giving and receiving of information. The missions
> have no direct military authority and therefore the proper procedure is not
> to beg them cap in hand for the material needed at air bases but to request
> them to supply us with what is needed to strengthen a movement that is
> operating in the immediate interest of the Allies.

Basil recalled:

> Our own orders at this stage were brief and clear about tasks to be carried
> out. So far as Genoa and its installations were concerned, these were to
> secure maximum effort by the CLN and its fighting units in an enterprise
> called anti-scorch. This meant the planning and eventual carrying out of
> actions to prevent enemy demolition of ports, railways, tunnels, public
> service installations and the rest.[5]

On 9 April, Peter delivered his orders to the members of the CLN, which amounted to the exact opposite of their 'Plan A'. Basil recalled: 'We were told to instruct the *Cichero* Divisions not to go down into the towns, and above all not to go down against the enemy in Genoa.' Remo Scappini, a Communist skilled worker who was President of the six-party Ligurian CLN, wrote in his memoir—entitled *Da Empoli a Genova (From Empoli to Genoa)*—that the mission made a 'drastic intervention' in the plans for insurrection:

[The mission wished] to clarify the attitude of the Allied High Command to the entry of partisan forces into Genoa and other cities. The principle to be observed in every case is the following: a minimal number of partisans must enter the city and remain there ... The principle was decisively rejected by the committee and its regional commanders.

As Basil related, the mission eventually worked out a compromise plan:

In a long radio message to the 5th Army, Peter recommended agreement on a rising within the city, aimed at anti-scorch, that would be backed by the rapid infiltration of 300 picked fighting men from the mountain units ... I cannot recall that we ever received any comments, favourable or otherwise, and the rising in Genoa began and then continued upon the quite different and altogether larger 'Plan A' of Miro's command. It stands on the record that British warships did in fact make a naval demonstration off Genoa on the third day of the insurrection. Though too late to be of any use, this was the Allies' sole contribution to the whole remarkable affair.[6]

Peter wrote that as early as 15 April, the German commander, General Gunther Meinhold, 'had made tentative approaches through the Cardinal of Genoa, suggesting that some agreement be reached whereby in return for his refusal to destroy public services, he would be allowed to withdraw his troops without molestation by the partisans'.

On 20 April, General Heinrich von Vietinghoff, the new German commander in Italy, issued his order to retreat across the River Po (codenamed 'Operation Autumn Mist'). General Meinhold was instructed to proceed as swiftly as possible along the valley and to make for the Veneto. On the morning of 23 April, Peter wrote:

... the General made a more definite approach to the Cardinal, saying that he needed three or four days in which to withdraw, and undertaking not to allow extensive demolitions. The Cardinal referred this to the CLN Liguria who replied that they would not treat with the enemy.

As night fell, the Liberation Committee ordered a general insurrection throughout the city of Genoa. At first light on Tuesday 24 April, the partisan rising began in Genoa and across Liguria. Towns north of the city and along the coast road fell to the partisans, the railway lines were cut, and public installations were secured.

Savage fighting raged in the centre of Genoa, around Piazza De Ferrari, and in the port. Seven thousand German troops and a similar number of Fascist soldiers and auxiliaries faced some 3,000 partisans. Two-thirds of the irregulars belonged to Communist formations, with the remainder in groups controlled by the Christian Democrat and Action parties. Peter related: 'The urban partisans (SAP) came out in force, secured arms from the enemy to reinforce the few they had already, and succeeded in cutting the main enemy groups off from each other.' Telephone wires and water and electrical supplies to the garrisons were severed, and transport was disabled. German columns were also blockaded in tunnels on the road to Milan, and their situation was deteriorating.

From his headquarters at Savignone, north of the city, General Meinhold issued a threat to order his artillery on Monte Moro and in the port to bombard the city unless his troops were allowed to retreat. The CLN decided to counter the ultimatum with one of its own: 'The moment a shell explodes in the city, we will execute the troops we have captured.' The enemy guns stayed silent. However, as Tuesday closed, the position of the partisans seemed perilous. The mountain formations were at least a day's march away, and the Americans had only just reached La Spezia—over 60 miles further down the coast. General mobilisation was ordered by the partisans in Genoa, and secret recruiting posts were set up in four different sectors. By daybreak, 3,000 civilians had been enrolled in a makeshift rebel army.

Orders had meanwhile been sent to the mountain units, and they began their march on the city. From the north-east, brigades *Balilla* and *Severino* came through the Bisagno and Polcevera valleys, and from the north-west the *Pio* and *Buranello* brigades moved down into Sestri Ponente and Sampierdarena. The Sixth Zone command received definite confirmation of the rumours of insurrection on 25 April, and, according to the agreed plan, certain units began to move on Genoa, while others opened up in full strength on the Scrivia Valley communications and down towards Route 1.

Shortly before midday, an ambulance from Genoa drove up to the German Headquarters at Savignone. Hidden in the back of the vehicle was a leading member of the Resistance—Carmine Romanzi of the Action Party. The partisan handed two letters to General Meinhold. One was from the CLN, and it demanded his surrender; the other was from Cardinal Archbishop Pietro Boetto of Genoa, in which he attempted to solicit a peaceful solution.

The General reluctantly agreed to meet the Liberation Committee and was driven to Genoa in the ambulance, led by two partisan outriders. The German handed Romanzi his pistol during the journey. Accompanying the General were his Chief of Staff, Captain Asmus, and a junior officer, Joseph Pohl, who acted as interpreter. They were taken to Cardinal Boetto's seat—the Villa Migone—at San Fruttuoso. Waiting at the residence were the German Consul, Von Hertzdorf, and the partisan representatives—the Communist Remo Scappini, Liberals Doctor Giovanni Savoretti and lawyer Errico Martino, and Major Mauro Aloni, military commander.

Negotiations began at 5 p.m. At around the same time, a large number of the enemy surrendered in the port. It was revealed during the discussions that the partisans now held 1,360 German prisoners. General Meinhold finally agreed to surrender. Remo Scappini related that after hours of indecision, the German signed (almost impetuously) at 7.30 p.m. The witnesses had the impression that he had carried out the most important duty of his life.

The surrender document reads:

It has been agreed that:

1. All the German Armed Forces on land and sea under the command of General Meinhold surrender to the Armed Forces of the CVL belonging to the Military Command of Liguria.
2. The surrender will be carried out by the troops giving themselves up to the nearest partisan units and handing over their weapons.
3. The Liguria CLN undertakes to treat the prisoners according to International Law, with special regard to their personal property and conditions of internment.
4. The Liguria CLN will consign the prisoners to the Allied Anglo-American command operating in Italy.

Four copies were made—two in Italian, two in German. Meanwhile, as Peter related:

Major Davidson with Attilio [Amino Pizzorno], now the Commissar of the Zone Command, set off from Torriglia to see how far they could get towards Genoa and rode right down into the centre of the city, past block after block posted by the suburban SAP, without hindrance except for sporadic sniping. Contact was made immediately with the Regional Command and with the CLN. Major Davidson found all the public services working and the newspapers on the point of going to press.

Local sources time Basil's arrival at the College of San Nicola (temporary home of the CLN and the military command) at 12.30 a.m. The Major heard of the enemy capitulation from Errico Martino, who said: 'The Germans have surrendered. To the CLN, to us.' The news was immediately signalled to Fifth Army Headquarters in Florence, though it was apparently never passed on to the advancing Americans in the 92nd Infantry Division.

The unit, nicknamed 'the Buffalo Soldiers', had been activated as the only black American infantry division in Europe (albeit with white senior officers). However, after months of fighting around the Gothic Line, only one black regiment remained in the division—the 370th. It was brought up to strength by the 473rd Regiment, made up of white anti-aircraft-gunners-turned-infantrymen, and by the motorised 442nd Regimental Combat team, formed from Nisei soldiers—descendants of Japanese immigrants. The 92nd was now affectionately known as the 'Rainbow Division'.

At 9 a.m. on Thursday 26 April, a prominent Christian Democrat, Paolo Emilio Taviani, reached the radio station at Granarolo and announced the surrender over *Radio Genova*. After reading the text of the capitulation, Taviani added:

> People of Genoa, rejoice! The insurrection, your insurrection has succeeded. For the first time in the course of the war a well-trained and well-armed army corps has surrendered to the people. Genoa is free. Long live the Genoese! Long live Italy!

However, considerable firing was still going on in the city. Peter recalled that large bodies of enemy troops were resisting, or at least they had not capitulated:

> General Meinhold had surrendered a few hours beforehand, but had made it clear that he could not answer for all his troops since he had now been out of touch with them for many hours. In fact several garrisons refused to acknowledge his orders. Colonel Klein, commanding some two thousand men in the port, actually held a court martial in which General Meinhold was condemned to death as a traitor.
>
> In the morning, the CLN held a solemn ceremony of investiture of the Prefect in the newly liberated Prefecture and Lieutenant-Colonel Davidson (whose promotion had been advised the night before) was invited to witness this. It was the first occasion upon which the whole CLN—consisting of eighteen members when non-party representatives are included—had met together in one place and recognised each other.
>
> Just as this rather moving ceremony was closing, news came in that all three major garrisons still resisting were in course of trying to force a junction, and it seemed the situation might be critical in view of the relatively tiny number of partisan troops in the city.

About 1,000 enemy troops succeeded in making their way westwards from the German Naval HQ at Nervi, as far as the skyscraper at the Foce di Bisagno, east of the port, and blockaded themselves in. Another 2,000 in the port made a bid to break out and were held. A third party (some 300 strong but surrounded in Sampiedarena) blew up a large ammunition dump, killing a substantial number of civilians, as a means of diversion while they tried to break out from an adjacent point. They too were held by reinforcements hurried down from Pontedecimo and Bolzaneto in any transport that could be found. By the afternoon, the position had greatly eased.

At about 4 p.m., Lieutenant-Colonel Davidson went with 'Miro' of the Zone Command and Colonel Farini of the Regional Command to induce the surrender of the 1,000 naval ranks at Foce di Bisagno. They undertook to surrender at 10 a.m. the following morning, which they did.

Meanwhile, the port garrison of 2,000—who were probably aware of the approach of Allied columns, by then already a short way west of Rapallo—thought better of their resistance; they surrendered unconditionally to partisan formations after throwing a large number of their arms into the water. No port installations were blown up, but several small block-ships had already been sunk. The remaining enemy positions—the batteries on Monte Moro and groups at Sampierdarena at Pontedecimo—held out until the following day.

Peter arrived at 11 p.m. and drove to meet the advancing Americans near Ruta. In the course of the morning of 27 April, troops began to flow into the city. The battle was over. The anti-scorch programme had been realised almost in its entirety. On that day, as previously, Genoa had light, water, public transport, newspapers, and radio transmissions from the local station, and the main roads prepared for destruction by the enemy were open.

A meeting between General Edward M. Almond, the commanding officer of the American 92nd Infantry Division, and the Liberation Committee took place at the Hotel Bristol at 1 p.m. Basil related that there was an initial misunderstanding:

'Tell them,' General Almond said, 'that my troops have liberated their city and they are free men.'

A silence followed: which continued.

The general looked at me with some surprise: couldn't I speak the language?

Then Providence intervened, or the sacred law, or whatever you prefer to think may now and then take pity on the frailties of humankind and stop collisions in the avenues of time. There came, from outside that room, the sudden din of shouts and uproar.

We rushed through the floor-to-ceiling windows to a balcony giving on that street of arcades.

Looking down, we saw far up the street the dense fore-ranks of a crowd of advancing men, and then we saw it was a column, a column of German prisoners a dozen or more abreast, hundreds of them, thousands of them, marching down that street unarmed but with armed partisans on either side ... At my elbow, General Almond said nothing, but he looked. The prisoners came on down that street, an endless column, for it turned out afterwards that more than 14,000 German and Fascist prisoners had been taken in Genoa alone. And the people in the arcades continued to clap and cheer.

Then we went back into the salon and General Almond gave me a measuring glance and said 'All right.' And then he made a speech that warmed the heart. He had known nothing of what to expect, but of this he said no word. Instead, he praised and thanked the CLN for what they and their troops had done.[7]

Peter wrote that the taking of Greater Genoa from the enemy and the more-or-less simultaneous liberation of the whole neighbouring territory was an achievement that perhaps astonished no one more than the very people who carried it out:

Many factors combined to make it possible. First among these was the almost complete disintegration of the enemy under the speed and success of the Allied advance, coming as it did on top of long and demoralising months of waiting in Italy while the German homeland was being invaded and overrun, and waiting, moreover, in a partisan infested country.

General Meinhold, commanding the fortress of Genoa, surrendered himself and all his troops virtually without resistance. Had he not done so, but had shared the die-hard views of some of his officers, there is no doubt he could have destroyed the public services of Genoa and caused severe losses to those who might have attacked him. Still, it is fair to add that an important factor in his decision to surrender, as indeed he admitted in conversation with us, was his certainty that his troops would be subject to sustained and general attack by partisans during retreat.

On Thursday 3 May, the day after the guns had fallen silent across Italy, a victory parade of partisans and American troops was held in Genoa. Over the next three weeks, Basil helped his friend write his report on Clover Mission. Peter's account ends on a typical note:

It would be ungracious to conclude this brief summary of events without some reference to the outstanding courtesy and kindness which I and the other members of my mission were shown after liberation by partisans of all ranks and formations. We were invited to numerous ceremonial occasions, directly or indirectly in our honour. At the end, on 16 May, together with Lieutenant-Colonel Davidson, Sergeant Armstrong, 'Captain Van' and the W/T operator of the OSS mission, and five partisan commanders, I was presented with the freedom of the City of Genoa. The name above mine in the city records reads 'Mussolini,' and that is being erased. Above that is Guglielmo Marconi.

The experience of war dissolved in such moving ceremonies across Italy, a symbolic ending and also the affirmation of ties that still endure.

13

Air Force Heroes

Secret aerial operations were usually the only method of contact with the interior. The missions kept the Resistance movement in touch with the Allies and provided evidence of concrete support. Weapons, supplies and agents were parachuted to partisan groups, and light aircraft landed on makeshift airstrips. Air supply also helped to keep escape lines open and maintain a network of agents in the field.

The covert operations were coordinated by the British SOE and the American OSS. Flights were also made for the British Special Air Service (SAS) and the Secret Intelligence Service (SIS), under its cover name of the Inter-Services Liaison Department; for the escape and evasion services, the British MI9 (with the cover name of IS9), and for the American MIS-X; and for the joint Psychological Warfare Board (PWB).

The establishment of Allied secret agencies and air units for special operations required unique command structures, as set out by Major Harris Gaylord Warren in a report on the part played by American airmen in support of the partisan movements:

> Activities undertaken by the allies to aid resistance groups and for espionage in enemy-occupied areas required an extensive organization. There were intelligence agencies, both British and American, which carried on secret work. These agencies were represented by personnel in enemy territory who cooperated with the underground groups. Allied air forces provided the planes and crews to transport agents, to deliver supplies, to drop propaganda leaflets, and to evacuate personnel. The closest liaison existed between the secret agencies and the air forces, and the success of the entire programme of special operations depended upon full cooperation. Special agencies determined policies, laid the plans, made complete arrangements for their execution, and then depended upon the air forces to bring them to fruition.[1]

Agents in enemy territory contacted OSS and SOE headquarters through special channels of communication regarding the requirements of air supply and the targets for deliveries. Liaison officers then presented the field demands to the air forces. Targets Sections on the airfields confirmed the drop zones and set loading arrangements and recognition signals. Through their ability to grant or to withhold supplies in this way, the Allies exercised a strong influence on the success or failure of the partisan forces.

The secret services allocated a codename to the area for the landing of troops or supplies and logged the coordinates. To alert the ground reception party, short and simple statements from a list authorised by the British Broadcasting Corporation were broadcast as personal messages at the end of the news on the Italian programme. A second signal was sent a few days later to confirm that the drop was imminent. Decisions on the suitability of weather conditions and targets remained with the commanding officers of the squadrons. One or two alternative drop zones were often provided, so as to increase the effectiveness of operations.

The security of Resistance members and Allied agents was a basic concern in these covert missions. From their point of view, it was desirable to have targets in hidden ravines wherever possible. These made low-level approaches at night extremely difficult, but drops were still made to zones within gorges in the Italian Alps, more than a mile below the peaks running no more than 2–3 miles on either side. The squadrons flew to the pinpoints repeatedly at night, even in the dark period of the moon. The enemy also set up false targets, with the result that great care had to be taken in identifying both the location of the site and the signal letter. There were a few instances when supplies were dropped to the Germans or Fascists despite the precautions.

Supplies were released when the plane was at a height of between 500 and 1,000 feet. The bulk of the goods were weapons and ammunition, including Sten guns and rifles, heavier arms such as bazookas, and occasionally a pack howitzer. In addition, mines and other demolition equipment and caps and fuses were landed. It was also necessary to carry non-combat stores essential to the sustenance of groups of men in the hills—especially food, clothing, boots, medical supplies, radio kits, flashlights and batteries.

A maximum load for a B-17 Flying Fortress consisted of sixteen containers and eight packages, and eighteen containers and six packages for a B-24 Liberator—the main aircraft used in the first part of the airlift. The Liberators deployed in special operations had minimal identification markings and were painted black. The ball turret was removed, and an opening just over 3 feet wide was cut in the floor for drops. Flame suppressors were placed on the engine exhausts, unnecessary items such as oxygen equipment were removed, and the gunners manning the two remaining turrets were ordered not to fire unless the aircraft itself came under attack.

Each container was a metal cylinder just over 1 foot in diameter and 5 feet 9 inches long, and they could carry up to 220 lbs—a four-man load. Gaps were filled with clothing and scarce goods such as coffee and tobacco. A few stores (like uniforms, blankets and boots) could be thrown from the plane without the need for holders or wrapping. An average load weighed 6,200 lbs. The containers were carried in the bomb bay except for two that were placed in the waist with the packages. Parachutes attached to a static line were fixed to both containers and packages. The containers were eased out by the bomb aimer while the packages were pushed out of the hatch well by the dispatcher on a light signal from the bomb aimer. Two or more runs were usually required over the target for an exact drop.

Agents sat beside the hatch and jumped out on a signal at a height of about 600 feet. A red light turned to green, the dispatcher's arm swept down as he shouted 'Go!', and the individual launched into space, springing to attention to avoid becoming entangled in the cords of the parachute as it was pulled open by the static line. The parachutist's departure was easier from one type of aircraft—the Douglas Dakota C-47 transporter, codenamed the DC-3 by the British. The agent simply jumped out of a door on the port side of the plane.

Navigation was a major problem for aircrews trying to find drop or landing zones identified only by flashlights or fires. The partisans typically instigated contact; the targets were initially marked with three lights in a line and with another on the side flashing a Morse letter to identify the site. The aircraft would occasionally initiate the signal by flashing a letter, but this practice was discouraged as it gave away its location and that of the target. In the later flights to Italy, the receptions were shaped in the form of rectangular letters, with an additional light flashing one or two letters of Morse. Daylight targets were marked with panels or parachutes placed in the form of a huge letter, occasionally accompanied by a smoking fire. As navigation was much more exact in the daylight, little difficulty was experienced in finding and identifying these sites.

A report would usually arrive from the field about the accuracy of the drop a week or so after it was made. The most common comment was one of gratitude for the supplies and thanks to the crew. Whenever an agent was parachuted, a report would come back quickly with the news that he had arrived safely.

One of the initial problems lay in training air crews. The men from bomb groups were experts in tight daylight formation flying, but they had little experience of night operations. Each aircraft was required to fly on its own and at low altitude to its special target in mountainous country. The pilots had to reduce the air speed to between 120 and 130 mph over the drop zone. Reliable electronic aids were almost non-existent, and so map reading and dead reckoning had to be used. As a result, the nights of major effort fell on the seventeen nights of each month that the moon provided sufficient light to see the terrain.

The weather was a constant obstacle during the long flights, and it frequently became necessary to fly through frontal conditions. In addition to the usual hazards of extreme turbulence and icing, cloud formations were not so recognisable at night, and the storm centre could not be easily identified. The effect known as St Elmo's fire would shoot bright blue and violet sparks from the wing tips, lighting up propellers like Catherine wheels and making the nose glow. At low altitude, clouds among the mountain peaks were a significant hazard.

The navigator's compartment was blacked out and the bomb aimer in the nose became the eyes for map reading. He carried 1:500,000 scale maps and dimmed flashlights. The most recognizable features were river junctions or bends, lakes, and mountains. Islands over the water leg made excellent references if not covered by stratus cloud. The coastline was also a checkpoint, though enemy flak often made it a dangerous one. The bomb aimer was of particular importance at the target because he prepared a large-scale overlay of the immediate target area, and not only guided the run but also identified the reception and released the bomb-bay load. He also signalled the dispatcher in the waist for the agent's jump or the dispatching of packages. From his blacked-out nose, the bomb aimer's vision was the best in the plane, and he became its eyes at night.

The aircraft maintained radio silence until it had crossed the enemy coast on return from a mission. The crew would then provide identification, specify success or failure, and give the expected time of return. The ground station sent periodic weather information and any necessary instructions. If an airfield had to be closed temporarily, the planes would be diverted to other bases.

By the end of 1944, most planes had a receiving scope (known as a 'Rebecca') in the navigator's compartment to indicate the direction and proximity of a radio beacon device on the ground called a 'Eureka'. The range of the sets was only about 30 miles, but they could be a valuable aid over the target and even allow drops through solid cloud. The system also helped ensure a safe return to base when used in conjunction with a radio range, light beacons and searchlights. However, results in the field were disappointing; only a minority of missions were equipped with the beacons, and the British Mark III sets proved unreliable. A complementary signals system known as an S-Phone also helped communication over the ground, but sets were again scarce and the system experienced similar operational problems to Eureka.

The tried-and-tested wireless telegraph remained the central element in coordinating aerial and ground activities. The operators were key members of missions to enemy territory. Following the Armistice of September 1943, the SOE signals station moved from North Africa to Brindisi before becoming established at the Monopoli base. Its final location was Siena, which was more convenient for collaboration with partisans in the field, and in February 1945 this provided the new base for both Special Operations Mediterranean (SOM) and SOE.

Fortunately, the rapid rise of the partisan movement coincided with the decision to give greater support to the Resistance and to move special air operations to Italy. Number 334 Wing RAF assumed control of special-duties flights in the Mediterranean in November 1943. The missions were initially flown from North Africa, but by the end of January 1944 all the formations had moved to Brindisi, Puglia, which became the centre of aerial operations in the Mediterranean.

The British Royal Air Force supplied 148 and 624 squadrons and 1586 Polish Flight. The USAAF 62nd Troop Carrier Group arrived in February. It used the versatile C-47 Douglas Dakota transporters, which gradually became the main aircraft used to ferry men and supplies. A flight of army co-operation and liaison aircraft—Westland Lysanders—arrived from Britain and was attached to 148 Squadron. In March, 267 Transport Command Squadron RAF brought its Dakotas to Brindisi. Two squadrons of the co-belligerent Italian Air Force based at Lecce were also placed under the wing's control. Number 624 Squadron was withdrawn to Blida, Algeria, in February to supply southern France, and it was disbanded in September.

On 1 June 1944, HQ Balkan Air Force became the controlling formation for all special operations carried out by Italian-based aircraft. Brindisi was home to 148 Squadron RAF, 1586 Polish Flight (from 7 November reformed as 301 Squadron), and the Dakotas of 64 Troop Carrier Group, USAAF. Bari was the base for 267 Squadron RAF and for a Russian Air Group, mainly supplying Yugoslavia. The squadrons of the co-belligerent Italian Air Force were based at Lecce. Finally, the Foggia group of airfields were home to the squadrons of Number 205 (Heavy Bomber) Group RAF, which was made available for mass supply operations in northern Italy when priority necessitated.

In September, the United States 885th Bombardment Squadron, which had been supplying the *Maquis* forces in France, was moved within Algeria from Blida to Maison Blanche, and then on to Brindisi, with a main commitment to supply the Italian Resistance movement. In November, Dakota formations of the USAAF 51st Troop Carrier Wing were made available for operations in Italy from bases in Tuscany, at Tarquinia and at Malignano (where there was a packing station). Supply operations were initially carried out by the 62nd Troop Carrier Group; however, it was replaced on 11 January by the 64th Troop Carrier Group, based at Rosignano (also in Tuscany).

Another United States heavy bombardment squadron, the 859th (nicknamed 'The Spooks'), arrived from the United Kingdom to reinforce the 885th at Brindisi in December 1944. The American aircraft mostly took over the Italian commitments while the RAF concentrated upon the Balkans, though arrangements were made so that all the aircraft could be deployed to either theatre depending upon the weather. The two American squadrons were formed into the small 15th Special Group (Provisional) on 20 January 1945. On 16 March the group joined units of the 51st Troop Carrier Wing, supplying the Italian partisans from Rosignano, Tuscany.

During the period in which special operations were carried out in Italy, a total of 4,280 sorties were flown, of which 2,652 (or 61.96 per cent) were successful. Five thousand nine hundred and seven tons of supplies were delivered, 538 agents were dropped by parachute, and 169 tons of leaflets were distributed on behalf of the Psychological Warfare Board (PWB). The Lysander pick-up operations also resulted in twenty-four men being brought out, as well as secret documents concerning enemy dispositions and intentions.

This is a breakdown of the activities of the formations, beginning with the RAF:

148 Squadron:	497 sorties, 299 successes, 897 tons of supplies dropped
1586 Polish Flight, later 301 Squadron:	305 sorties, 173 successes, 490 tons of supplies dropped
267 Squadron:	261 sorties, 129 successes, 258 tons of supplies dropped
624 Squadron:	42 sorties, 29 successes, 45 agents parachuted to escaped prisoners of war, 4 tons of supplies dropped
205 Group:	210 sorties, 156 successes, 250 tons of supplies dropped

Westland Lysanders made twelve sorties and had six successes. The Dakotas of the USAAF 51st Troop Carrier Wing carried out 1,933 sorties, of which 1,261 were successful, and 2,522 tons of supplies were dropped. The 885th and 859th squadrons of the USAAF Group made 1,020 sorties, with 599 successes and 1,486 tons of supplies dropped.

The military value of the work of the squadrons involved in secret aerial missions was infinitely greater than that accomplished by any similar number of heavy bombers. The human cost of the airlift is demonstrated in the next chapter.

14

Missing in Action

On 12 October 1944, two of the eight squadrons of Number 205 Heavy Bomber Group RAF flew a large-scale supply mission to northern Italy. As we have seen, the group conducted 210 such operations during the war, in addition to their combat role. One hundred and fifty-six of the missions were successful, and 250 tons of supplies were delivered to the partisans.

Between 4.05 and 4.40 p.m., twenty Liberators from 31 and 34 squadrons of the Second Wing of the South African Air Force (SAAF) lumbered into the sky above the air base of Celone, 6 miles north of Foggia in Puglia. The sortie reports note that they were 'supply dropping in northern Italy.' The operation had already been postponed on several occasions due to bad weather. The airfield was still flooded in places, but it was judged serviceable enough for the mission to take place. It was thought to be routine and there had been no losses of personnel over Italian targets.

Sixteen of the planes were flown by 31 Squadron, with one having to be borrowed from 34 Squadron. They in turn flew four aircraft. Usually both formations contributed equally to missions, but this time a maximum effort was required of the 31st. The officers of the 34th were holding a dance in Foggia that evening to celebrate the return of one of their comrades to South Africa. The eight-man crews were from South Africa, the United Kingdom and Australia.

The Liberators were assigned in groups of five to four coded target areas. Three were in Piedmont: Parrot, near Vigone, south-west of the regional capital, Turin; Dodge, south-east of the city, close to Bra; and Chrysler, in the lower Toce Valley, north-west of Lake Maggiore. The fourth drop zone (DZ) was Morris, near Neirone, north-east of Genoa, in the Ligurian Apennines. Each of the planes carried a dozen 150-kg (331-lb) canisters in their bomb bays, crammed with light machine guns, ammunition, hand grenades, radio equipment, food, and medical supplies.

Weather conditions on the day were worse than forecast. A depression arrived early and the Liberators flew into dense cloud. To the north of Elba and over north-western Italy, the aircraft also experienced problems in using the GEE radio navigation system due to technical problems of coverage. The crews were forced to mainly rely on 'dead reckoning'—that is, calculating a current position by using a previously determined fix and advancing it based upon known or estimated speeds over elapsed time and course. This was especially dangerous in areas surrounded by high mountains. Only a few of the crews were able to glimpse reference points on the ground during transient gaps in the clouds.

Two planes returned early. Liberator 156 Q of 34 Squadron, flown by Lieutenant Jan Maritz and with the target of Morris, arrived at 9.10 p.m., after only four hours and twenty-five minutes in the air. The sortie report records that it was impossible to identify ground features owing to the very poor visibility. The aircraft was followed thirty-five minutes later from the Parrot DZ by EW 279 V, piloted by Lieutenant Reginald Franklin of 31 Squadron. The sortie report notes: 'The captain decided to return to base, being unable to identify ground detail through 10/10 cloud.' The War Diary of 31 Squadron noted: 'These conditions, coupled with no GEE facilities, rendered the necessary accurate navigation in the mountainous areas well-nigh impossible.'

As we saw in Chapter 8, on the Free Zone of Ossola, two of the planes bound for DZ Chrysler were successful in dropping their supplies to the beleaguered partisans despite the weather conditions. South African Captain Bill Senn, of 31 Squadron, piloted Liberator KH 205 Y. Contact was able to be made with the ground reception party. Another 31 Squadron pilot, Australian Flying Officer Max Badham, flew EW 158 G with an RAF crew. In this case, ground signals were confusing but the local topography was positively identified.

By midnight on 12–13 October, fourteen Liberators had returned to Celone; however, eleven had been unable to deliver their supplies. An anxious wait began for the remaining six planes. In the morning there was only bright and empty sky. A long list of airmen who had not returned appeared on the Mess notice board. No radio contact could be established with the aircraft, and none had landed at emergency airfields.

Reports soon came through from partisans in Piedmont that two of the Liberators had crashed in the mountains with the loss of all those on board. KH 154 W of 31 Squadron, piloted by Australian Flight Sergeant Desmond Watson, age twenty, had been bound for DZ Dodge, but it crashed on Monte Cornur, in the Commune of Rorà. Liberator KH 239 S, flown by Flight Sergeant Clarence Lawton, Royal Australian Air Force (RAAF), age twenty-three, had crashed on Monte Freidour, near Cantalupa. He was from 31 Squadron, while the crew were from 34 Squadron—all RAF. The aircraft had been assigned to the nearby DZ of Parrot.

Three more crash sites were found in more inaccessible areas at the end of the war. The planes had all been captained by South Africans of 31 Squadron. Liberator KG 874 J, flown by Lieutenant Alexander Metelerkamp and sent to Dodge, hit the hillside above Ostana. The lieutenant, age twenty-three, was from Stellenbosch, Cape Province, and had joined the SAAF two years earlier as a student.

The other two planes were bound for Chrysler. Liberator KG 999 P of 31 Squadron left Celone at 4.15 p.m. The First Pilot was Lieutenant Charles Nel, from Oudtshoorn, Cape Province; at twenty-one he was the youngest heavy bomber pilot in the SAAF. He joined 31 Squadron at Lydda, Palestine, in March 1944, as they were preparing to convert from Douglas Bostons to Consolidated Liberators. The mission of 12 October 1944 was his twenty-third; he had just received his own command in September.

The other members of the crew were: Sergeant Jack Boswell, twenty-one, second pilot, RAF; Lieutenant Coen Vorster, twenty-nine, navigator, SAAF; Lieutenant Ronald Johnson, twenty-one, bomber, RAF; Sergeant Eric Lockey, twenty, radio operator and air gunner, RAF; Sergeant Henry Foy, twenty-one, radio operator and air gunner, RAF; Sergeant Roy Bailey, nineteen, air gunner, RAF; and Sergeant Harry Austin, twenty-four, air gunner, RAF.

At 8.30 p.m., just over four hours after take-off, KG 999 P was overflying the Lanzo Valley, approximately 25 miles north-west of Turin. The valley was shrouded in mist. Residents were indoors due to a curfew. They heard the thundering roar of the plane overhead, followed by a rumbling sound from the direction of the Punta del Rous Mountain (2,535 metres). A sudden flash cut through the gloom, and then there was silence.

Three British escapers were embedded with the local *Garibaldi* brigade—Private Herbert Wood of the Second Queen's Own Cameron Highlanders and his companions, Eric and Norman. Herbert submitted a crash report to MI9:

> We heard a low flying aircraft. There was fog and we could not see it. The engines seemed to be running normally. Later we saw a glow in the sky which we took to be flares. We heard no noise of an explosion. However, the following day we learned that an aircraft had crashed. Weather prevented us from getting out to search for wreckage until 16 October.[1]

The Britons accompanied the partisans on the four-hour ascent to the peak. They found that the bomber had failed to clear the mountain by only about 10 yards. The burnt wreckage was scattered on the crest and as far as 50 yards below. From clothing, Bren guns and rifles near the aircraft, it became apparent that the aircraft had been on a supply mission. The weapons and ammunition were salvaged by the partisans.

Bad weather prevented the recovery of the bodies of the crew members until 23 October, when they were taken to the village of Ceres for burial. The villagers sent wreaths and flowers, the partisans provided a firing party, and the service was conducted by the local priest. There was no time to place a cross because a party of Germans arrived and everyone had to disperse in a hurry. Ten partisans were said to have been captured. The personal effects of some of the crew allowed the identification of the Liberator, and these were taken over the border to the Allies in France by the three British soldiers in December 1944.

On 2 June 2002 the Italian authorities held a ceremony at Ala di Stura to remember the sacrifice of those young men, placing a bronze plaque commemorating them at Punta del Rous. The monument was bolted onto a large, sloping rock on the mountainside, near the plane's point of impact. Eight family members of the crew from South Africa and the United Kingdom took part in the ceremony.

Liberator KG 875 D left Celone at 4.15 p.m., the same time as KG 999 P. The First Pilot was South African Captain Leonard von Solms Beukes, age twenty-six, from Petrusburg in the Free State. He joined the SAAF in January 1940, becoming an instructor and then being posted to 31 Squadron in April 1944.

The Second Pilot was Sergeant George Anstee, RAF, age twenty-three, from Gloucestershire. He left grammar school at sixteen and joined the Air Force as a boy entrant at the same time as his older brother, Victor. George received his training at the RAF station in Shoeburyness, and he was serving at RAF Lee-on-Solent in 1940, when it was attacked by German bombers. The following year, he was posted to RAF Luqa in Malta (the last time his family saw him) and promoted to Sergeant. In the summer of 1943, after the siege of the island was lifted, George was sent to Salisbury in the British colony of Southern Rhodesia to train as a pilot; he eventually joined 31 Squadron SAAF for service in the Mediterranean.

The rest of the crew were: Lieutenant Michiel Kruger, twenty-nine, navigator, SAAF; Sergeant Charles Foster, twenty-four, bomb aimer, RAF; Sergeant Hubert Woods, twenty, wireless operator and air gunner, RAF; Lieutenant Gavin Shipman, twenty-seven, SAAF, air gunner; Warrant Officer Derek Francis, twenty-four, air gunner, SAAF; and Sergeant William Pryce, twenty, wireless operator and air gunner, RAF.

At the end of the war, an American patrol was sent to investigate reports by civilians of a crashed Allied plane. The troops climbed the trail from the village of Pianetto, a hamlet within the commune of Valprato Soana, to the heights of the Arlens Valley. They found traces of the aircraft here. The intelligence section of Mediterranean Allied Air Forces reported to 31 Squadron:

People in Pianetto say that at 20.00 on 12 October this plane flew over them and they heard it crash in the mountains. The walking trail from Pianetto to the scene of the crash is most difficult. Not the remotest possibility of mules navigating it.

It was apparent that the aircraft had blown up, because wreckage was scattered for several hundred yards. From insignia recovered at the site, the squadron's Senior Intelligence Officer identified the wearer as Captain von Solms Beukes, and therefore the plane as KG 875 D.

On 27 July 2013, a memorial service to the airmen was held in the church at Pianetto, attended by relatives from the United Kingdom and South Africa. A monument was placed in the square as the national anthems were played by an *Alpini* band. A group also ascended to the crash site, only 100 yards below the summit, and erected a cross and a smaller version of the plaque. Translated, it reads:

> In memory of the crew of Liberator KG 875 of 31 Squadron of the South African Air Force, which crashed in the Arlens Valley on 12 October 1944 during a supply mission to the forces of the Resistance.

Forty-eight airmen were lost on this one night—forty from 31 Squadron and eight from the 34th. Some of the aircraft on the mission had faced flak as they crossed the coastline near Genoa, but generally it was light and lasted less than a minute. Enemy fighters had been withdrawn in September, so the cause of the tragedy probably lies in the perils of flying in submission to what the ill-starred French aviator and writer Antoine de Saint-Exupéry called 'those elemental divinities—night, day, mountain, sea and storm'. The 31 Squadron War Diary notes:

> It was felt that the only explanation could be a determination on the pilots' part to drop the supplies successfully—and in order to do so the aircraft had lost height to break cloud and collided with surrounding high features.

Adverse weather conditions also seriously interfered with supply missions flown to northern Italy by the American squadrons at night. The 885th Bombardment Squadron flew eighty-five sorties on the seven operational nights during October. Only thirty-three were successful, and two B-24 Liberators were lost.

One of the twenty heavy bombers to take off from Celone airfield on the afternoon of 12 October 1944 was never seen again. Liberator KH 158 H of 31 Squadron left at 4.15 p.m. for the Morris drop zone, the only target in Liguria. The First Pilot was South African Major Selwyn Urry, twenty-nine. The rest of the crew were Lieutenants Norman Armstrong, air gunner, and Geoffrey Collard, nineteen, navigator; Second Lieutenant Peter Lordan, air gunner; and Warrant Officer Leonhard Bloch, twenty-one, air gunner, all SAAF; Flying Officer George Hudspith, second pilot; and Sergeant Reginald Fitzgerald, nineteen, air gunner, both RAF; and Flying Officer Thomas Roberts Millar, twenty-eight, RAAF, observer and bomb aimer.

The intended recipients of the weapons and supplies were the *Garibaldi* formations of the *Cichero* Division, which controlled a large part of the mountains of the Fontanabuona Valley. The remaining four of the five planes assigned to Morris were from 34 Squadron. As we have seen, Liberator 156 Q, piloted by Lieutenant Jan Maritz, was the first to return early to Celone. Liberator 207 K, piloted by Sergeant David Burry, and 153 P, flown by Flight Sergeant Trevor Foram, both reached the target but were unable to deliver supplies due to the very poor visibility. Liberator 204 C, flown by Captain Selby David Marsh, was credited with 'a partial success'.

The sortie report for the remaining aircraft, KH 158 H—the only one from 31 Squadron directed to the Morris DZ—simply says 'aircraft and crew missing'. Mrs Anne Storm, the Australian daughter of Flying Officer Thomas Roberts Millar, has conducted a rigorous investigation in an attempt to solve the mystery of the plane's disappearance.

Anne's father, known to family and friends as 'Bob', was born in the small town of Narromine, New South Wales, Australia, on 7 September 1916. He graduated from Sydney University in 1939 with a Bachelor of Economics degree and then obtained an administrative position with the Sydney Gaslight Company. In January 1942, Bob married Elizabeth ('Beth') Thompson before enlisting in the Royal Australian Air Force on 22 May as a volunteer. Their daughter, Anne, was born on 3 February 1943.

After initial training in Australia, Bob was commissioned on 4 February and came to the United Kingdom to receive further instruction. In January 1944 he was transferred to Italy and joined 104 Squadron, 205 Group RAF, at Foggia Main air base. He took part in sorties to northern Italy, Yugoslavia, Austria, Hungary and Romania.

In August, Bob was seconded as leading bomb aimer to 31 Squadron, South African Air Force, stationed at Celone air base, Foggia. Soon, he was making night flights in Liberator bombers to Warsaw as part of the campaign to drop supplies to the beleaguered partisans who had risen against the German occupation forces. The cost of the airlift was tragically high in men and machines, and ultimately it did not prevent the surrender of the Polish Resistance on 2 October.

Anne was just one year old when her father took part in the mission of 12 October 1944. She writes:

The wreckages of the crashed planes were eventually found, but there was no news of the sixth Liberator. The crew members of KH158 H, with Bob among the crew, were officially posted as missing in action—a sad ending for brave men. The disappearance of KH 158 H has yet to be solved.[2]

A search for the plane was launched in April 2006 in Lake Bolsena, Lazio, under the patronage of the British Embassy in Rome and the support of the Italian authorities. The flight path of the Liberators lay only 25 miles west, over the Tyrrhenian Sea, before the course was set for Elba and northern Italy. A remotely operated vehicle (ROV) from the British Ministry of Defence combed a section of the lake's bed and transmitted images to its parent craft on the surface. There are aircraft submerged in the lake, but nothing was discovered on the first day, and on the second the ROV became entangled in the wreck of a helicopter. The hunt had to be abruptly cancelled.

Anne visited the area of the Morris drop zone for the first time in the summer of 2001, together with her husband, Roy, and daughter, Elizabeth. It is located halfway between Rocca Cavallina and Monte Caucaso. Though not far from the sea, the zone is very mountainous, and it is only accessible with a four-wheel-drive vehicle.

On 15 May 2011 the last mission of Liberator KH 158 H was commemorated within the drop zone. The event was organised with the help of Italians Sandro Vazon and Beppe Barbero and took place in the mountains above Neirone at a stone dwelling, Faggio Rotondo, which was the wartime headquarters of the local partisans. It is now home to an Italian couple and a point on a hiking trail—the Alta Via dei Monti Liguri. A marble plaque listing the names of the crew was unveiled on the outside wall of a roundhouse in the grounds by Anne and by South African Martin Urry, the nephew of the pilot, Major Selwyn Urry.

The crews of every one of the planes lost on 12 October 1944 have now been remembered in moving ceremonies in northern Italy: October 2000 at Ostana (KG 874 J); April 2001 in Bra (KG 874 J and KH 154 W); June 2002 at Ala di Stura (KG 999 P); May 2011 in Neirone (KH158 H); July 2013 at Valprato Soana (KG 875 D); and September 2013 in Cantalupa (KH 239 S). The flags of Italy, South Africa, the United Kingdom, and Australia have been raised in the little villages in the mountains, and residents have joined local dignitaries and family members from overseas in services of remembrance and the installation of permanent memorials to the airmen. Two services have also been held in memory of Sergeant Reginald Fitzgerald, RAF, air gunner on KH 158 H, at the Parish of All Saints Church in his home village of Stapleford, Kent. His name has been added to the local war memorial and a street has been named 'Fitzgerald Close' in his honour.

Anne writes:

Liberator KH 158 H is still missing, but I feel that the placing of the plaque at the drop zone was the culmination of years of research into my father's wartime life and disappearance. Now more local Italian people and officials know about the loss of the plane and one day someone just might find information about its whereabouts. Did it go into the sea, explode in the air or crash in a remote mountain area? The search goes on![3]

Wartime aircraft posted as missing are still being recovered in Italy from land and sea.

15

A Wartime Romance

Frederick Lionel Rippingale (known to his colleagues as 'Rip') was born in London on 20 September 1916 and educated at Erith County School. He joined the RAF Volunteer Reserve in 1939 and was commissioned following training as an observer-navigator. In early 1941, Frederick attended 13 Operational Training Unit (OTU) Bicester and took part in bombing raids on the Dutch and German coasts. On 17 June he flew to Alexandria, via Gibraltar and Malta, to join 45 Squadron RAF (known as the 'Flying Camels') in the Western Desert campaign. His Bristol Blenheim light bomber, T2318, was shot down by a Messerschmitt Bf 109 while returning from a sortie near the Italian air force base of El Adem, in north-eastern Libya, on 22 November.

The pilot, Sergeant Pat Melly, and Frederick, the observer, were injured and captured by the Italians. The wireless operator and air gunner, twenty-six-year-old Sergeant John Halsall, was killed. Frederick was injured in the arm and shoulder and badly burned. He spent four months in hospital before being sent to a series of prisoner of war camps.

On the announcement of the Armistice on 8 September 1943, Frederick was one of twenty RAF men among the prisoners of war held at PG 49 Fontanellato, near Parma. He appears within the nominal role as a Pilot Officer. At noon on 9 September, the prisoners fled the camp shortly before the arrival of a German column sent to capture them. The men were anxious to leave the open plain of the River Po and moved into the nearby hills. Frederick and his companions joined a group of partisans near Borgo Val di Taro. Among their helpers was an attractive young woman called Maria Berni, who belonged to a family from the hill town of Bardi, which had Welsh connections. Frederick joined partisan raids against the Germans until the autumn of 1944. Once the front stabilised, he moved south and crossed enemy lines to the Americans of the 5th Army in November.

Frederick was repatriated to England and rejoined his parents at the family home in Belvedere. He subsequently accepted an invitation by SOE to return to Italy and act as a link with the partisans in the final stages of the war. Frederick was promoted to Flight Lieutenant and trained in sabotage, subversion and parachuting; he was then dropped behind enemy lines.

On the afternoon of 23 March 1945, the mission (codenamed 'Insulin') landed safely at an OSS-controlled pinpoint south of Santo Stefano d'Aveto, about 47 miles north-east of Genoa. The commanding officer was Captain Charles Brown of the Intelligence Corps; Frederick was his second in command. The wireless operator was Corporal Bradley of the Royal Corps of Signals. The next day, the trio reached the hamlet of Alpepiana and the headquarters of the Senior Liaison Officer for Liguria and Western Emilia, Lieutenant-Colonel Peter McMullen. The mission's area of operation was to be the Thirteenth Partisan Zone of Piacenza, with the specific duty of liaison with partisans of the Arda Valley, who were led by Lieutenant Giuseppe Prati. The senior mission for the province was commanded by Major Stephen Hastings. Codenamed 'Clover Two', it had landed at Santo Stefano on 2 February and was attached to the provincial partisan headquarters, known as the *Comando Unico* (CU). They were based at Groppallo, a small village nestling in the trees and mountains at the head of the Nure Valley.

The Colonel noted that to begin with there was scarcely one formation left in anything resembling fighting trim:

> Personal quarrels, always present below the surface, erupted in all directions. The zonal command was not only scattered about the countryside, broken up and in hiding, what was perhaps worse, its loss was regarded by most of the formation leaders as an advantage. They asked us to help them to form a new one. In the end it was gradually possible to help to bring some order and purpose out of this chaos ... so that, by April 1945, it proved possible for us to meet the orders of 15th Army Group for an all-out effort.[1]

Frederick was briefed to find suitable landing grounds in the province and to visit partisan formations. It was envisaged that drop-off and pick-up operations would be conducted by small Westland Lysander aircraft. They were painted matt black and modified to carry up to two agents or wounded personnel in addition to documents and supplies. The planes usually operated within a week of the full moon, and the pilots navigated by map and compass. The aircraft could land on short strips of land lit by torches. The runways needed little preparation.

The members of the new mission crossed the mountains to the province of Piacenza with Peter McMullen, meeting Stephen Hastings at Ferriere, in the Nure Valley, on 28 March to formulate plans. He recalled: 'The partisan units were far too scattered for us to ensure adequate control as things hotted up and we were all much relieved to get this extra help.' Stephen was now able to concentrate on liaison with the CU and with the other two main formations in the province—the *Prima Divisione Piacenza*, led by Fausto Cossu, and the *Valnure*, commanded by Pio Godoli ('Renato').

The Insulin agents were to assist the *Valdarda* Division, which was being reformed after the enemy offensive. On 30 March the mission met Lieutenant Prati and his staff in the valley at Sperongia. The division was composed of four brigades—the 141st, the 142nd, the 38th, and the *1st Oltre Po*—plus two detachments (with one made up of Russian deserters from the German Army). There were about 835 partisans. They were reasonably well-armed with Brens, machine guns and some bazookas, but lacked adequate boots and clothing. The mission reported that divisional morale was fairly good, but they lacked in offensive spirit after a very rough time from the enemy during the severe winter.

Another partisan formation of about 300 men—the *62nd Brigata Luigi Evangelista*—operated on the right bank of the Arda torrent. It was led by Emilio Varani, and it was temporarily under the control of the CU. Before the start of the enemy roundup in December 1944, the brigade had been commanded by an escaped prisoner of war, Yugoslav Lieutenant Jovan B. Gravac, who had fled from PG 26 Cortemaggiore after the Armistice. The Italians called him 'Giovanni lo Slavo' ('John the Slav'). The formation was lavishly armed by the OSS. Frederick knew the area well— these hills on the border with the province of Parma had been his first refuge after escaping from PG 49 Fontanellato in September 1943.

The mission made plans for the collection of intelligence, minor sabotage, and the safeguarding of strategic assets in the event of a German withdrawal. Attacks on enemy garrisons, petrol and ammunition dumps, transport and communications were stepped up, especially between the Via Emilia and the River Po. Captured enemy soldiers were interrogated and a small number of Italians were employed by the mission to collect intelligence.

Frederick was now on the move around the area to find landing strips. This involved a great deal of marching. Transport was difficult to obtain, particularly as vehicles on the roads invited strafing by United States daylight fighters (I write this with feeling, as my mother was attacked on her cycle). The partisan-controlled area was mostly mountainous or hilly, and it therefore did not seem to offer many suitable sites for aircraft to land. The military airport at San Damiano, in the commune of San Giorgio, seemed the best prospect, though it was only 10 miles south of Piacenza. From 1942 to 1944, the field had been expanded and used by the *Luftwaffe* for training its pilots; however, from the middle of 1943 it had come under attack from Allied bombers, culminating in two raids in May 1944 that rendered parts of the airport inoperative.

The mission made several trips over the mountains to Bardi, in the province of Parma, to visit an OSS Mission. Codenamed 'Cayuga', it was an Operational Group under the command of Captain Michael Formichelli, known to the

Italians as '*Roberto*'. The Americans had been parachuted on 27 December 1944 with the responsibilities of liaising with the Parma provincial command, targeting enemy communications, collecting intelligence, and training the partisans in sabotage. The group received and distributed seventy-six airdrops of supplies—some to formations on the border with Piacenza. The soldiers had instructions to cooperate with other Allied teams they might encounter, and they held regular meetings with the Insulin Mission to arrange liaison and exchange information.

The British missions worked hard on welding the diverse partisan groups into a coherent force that could descend into the plain and launch an attack on the city of Piacenza. This involved supporting and enhancing the authority of the central command at Groppallo. A potent weapon in the campaign was the declaration that supplies would only be distributed to formations loyal to the leadership. The first airdrops of containers and packages, blankets, and boots arrived at the partisan headquarters in March.

The *Valdarda* Division was in fair shape and undertaking coordinated actions by 1 April. Morale was good, and discipline was improving. Brigades had taken up clearly defined areas, established effective liaison with one another, and responded to the directions of the CU at Groppallo. The formations were pleased with the existence of a British mission in their area, and political problems did not crop up. The partisans said that they considered themselves as soldiers and intended to operate on military lines.

On 5 April, the signal came to mount an all-out effort. On the same day, the 62nd brigade (by now part of the division again) joined the 38th brigade in defeating an attempt by a company of seventy enemy troops—mainly Germans—to destroy the bridge at Castell'Arquato, which links the village to the Via Emilia. The soldiers were dispersed, the bridge was secured, and two armoured cars and many prisoners were taken.

On 16 April, two aircraft made the first drop specifically for the *Valdarda* division for almost a year, followed by another two days later. The supplies included weapons, ammunition, clothing and boots. Meanwhile, the search continued to find suitable landing strips. An engineer was sent to visit Lugagnano and San Damiano, while Frederick was looking for fields elsewhere. In the event, it was discovered that a detachment of sappers from the German Army had recently destroyed all the structures at San Damiano airport and that it was in ruins. The reconstruction of the airport began in 1952; ever since then, the airport has been the base for various formations of the Italian Air Force.

In the middle of April 1945, two Russian officers and fifty of their legionaries serving in the 162nd German Infantry Division of the Fourteenth Army deserted and joined the partisans. The new recruits were sent to join attacks on the enemy in a castle at Montechino and at nearby Gropparello.

The division moved in at the appointed time, but they found that the positions had already been abandoned. Offensives were launched on German outposts along the Via Emilia. After two or three days, the stretch of the highway between Pontenure and Fidenza was clear and the partisan forward positions reached the edge of the plain. In the Arda Valley the partisan HQ was moved down to Rustigazzo, and the Insulin Mission came with them. Meanwhile, Frederick was visiting various locations to look for airstrips; after a meeting on the subject with Stephen, he left to visit a site on the border with Liguria.

On 23 April, news came in that Fascist chiefs in Piacenza had packed their bags and that some had already fled. Two days later, the partisan command and Stephen's mission travelled down the Nure Valley to coordinate the offensive. Captain Charles Brown joined him at Bettola and received orders for the attack on Piacenza. He marched to Rustigazzo overnight and passed on the orders to Commandant Prati at 8.30 a.m. Messengers were sent to the brigades, and the whole division was on the move before noon.

The Fifth Army's breakthrough into the Po Valley had begun on 20 April. At dawn the next day, the Americans occupied Bologna—the regional capital of Emilia. One after another, the cities along the Via Emilia fell—Modena on the 21st, Reggio Emilia on the 24th, Parma on the 25th, and Fidenza on the 26th. Contrary to Hitler's final orders, General Heinrich von Vietinghoff authorised a general retreat to the line of the River Po. The city of Piacenza, on its right bank, was at the centre of the new deployment.

The Clover Two mission made contact with the advancing American 135th Infantry Division on 26 April through an SOE liaison officer, Captain Hugh McDermot, who crossed the lines in a scout car. Stephen visited the American headquarters in a captured German open staff car. He recalled: 'No one seemed to know that the mountains, and indeed all the approaches to Piacenza, belonged to the partisans.'

Charles left Rustigazzo with one of the partisans and marched overnight to meet Stephen at Pontenure, on the plain about 6 miles south-east of Piacenza, after ordering Frederick and Corporal Bradley to join him. In the afternoon, Charles visited the partisan units in an armoured car. They were within yards of the city walls, from where the enemy was firing artillery, mortars and machine guns. From then on, the Insulin Mission operated 'with and under the orders of Major Hastings'.

On 27 April the British received the signal 'Eighth and Fifth armies have broken through. Attack and hold Piacenza'. However, partisan patrols inside the city reported the presence of the remnants of an SS battalion, armed with ten armoured cars. Stephen requested the help of the Americans, but they refused. He related, 'They needed their tanks elsewhere, they said, and made clear they were content to leave Piacenza to the partisans.'

The Americans relented on 28 April and provided three Sherman tanks:

At seven o'clock in the morning we and our partisans went in with their support. There was not much resistance. The armoured cars disappeared after a few ineffective shots and by the morning of the 29th the SS and their Fascist friends had fled. Piacenza was ours. Moreover the partisans had saved the power and water supply. Both were working when the city was liberated.[2]

The partisans were speedily demobilised and an Allied Military Governor appointed for the province of Piacenza, Major Lewis J. McIntyre, US Army. My student mother, Clara Dall'Arda, was his interpreter. Frederick remained in Italy until July 1945. Resplendent in RAF uniform, he married his beautiful wartime helper, Maria Berni, in her home village of Bardi on the second of the month. The happy couple made a new life in England.

Major Stephen Hastings was awarded the Military Cross for his work in Piacenza. The citation noted that he was constantly to the fore, coolly directing and encouraging his men while under relentless mortar and machine-gun fire. Flight Lieutenant Rippingale was appointed MBE in the military division on 1 June 1945 in recognition of his services since his escape from captivity at Fontanellato on 9 September 1943. After SOE debriefing and demobilization in December, he returned to his pre-war employment with the Royal Dutch Shell Group.

16

The Allied Battalion

In December 1944, Major Roy Farran was sent to Italy as commandant of the newly raised Number 3 Squadron, 2nd Special Air Service (SAS) Regiment. The intention was to launch raids in support of the coming assault on the Gothic Line, making use of the mountainous terrain and the opportunity to cooperate with partisan forces.

His first move was to ask the commanding officer of Special Force Tactical Headquarters (TAC HQ) in Florence, Major Charles Macintosh, to sound out the British Liaison Officers in the provinces of Parma, Reggio and Modena for their reaction to receiving an SAS company in their areas. The most enthusiastic response was from Captain Michael ('Mike') Lees of the Envelope Mission in Reggio, and it was decided that the SAS force would be dropped to him. He had signalled: 'Send as many as you can!'

Mike Lees, who had already served as an SOE agent in Yugoslavia and northern Italy, had parachuted on 2 January 1945 to the snow-covered drop zone above Case Balocchi, at the foot of Mount Cusna. An enemy offensive began five days later, but when the enemy troops eventually withdrew he convened a meeting with the partisan provincial commandant, Augusto Berti ('Colonel Monti'), and other leaders at Febbio. Mike related that a plan was agreed, according to which:

> The partisans would be responsible to the *Comando Unico* as regards administrative matters, but for all operational questions, sabotage and tactical command, they would be responsible to me personally. All Intelligence would come direct to the mission. Political disturbances would not be tolerated. Finally, all brigades would be treated equally as purely military formations. Material from supply drops would be stored centrally and distributed fairly.

The Captain set about organising a protection and sabotage squad and a private intelligence service. He asked an *Alpini* officer called Glauco Monducci

('Gordon', after Flash Gordon) to build the forty-man squad. He named it the '*Gufo Nero*' or 'Black Owl', seeing the nocturnal predator as the perfect symbol for the partisan who also had to live and survive in the mountains. Intelligence was coordinated by a young partisan, Giulio Davoli ('Kiss'), who recruited a team of girls and young women to carry messages and orders and to cycle into the towns and bring back detailed information on enemy strength and dispositions. On 6 February the Colonel also ordered a former Air Force sergeant called Annibale Alpi, known as '*Barbanera*', to build a new unit that would be named the 'Military Formation'. It was directly under the command of the headquarters and open to partisans of every background.

Charles Macintosh recalled that his main preoccupation with the choice of Reggio for the SAS operation was that Roy would 'outrank Lees, who was the most impatient and headstrong of the BLOs'. He related: 'Together they could be a bloody menace—I consoled myself with the thought that it was the Hun who should be worried.'

The advance party of six SAS men parachuted to the Case Balocchi field on 4 March in Operation Tombola. Contrary to orders, they were led in person by Roy Farran, under the alias of 'Major McGinty'. The official report said that he 'was helping dispatch the men from the door of one of the Dakotas, overbalanced and fell'. Fortunately, this assistant dispatcher was wearing a parachute. Roy was billeted with the Envelope Mission in the priest's house at Secchio. An early meeting was held with 'Colonel Monti', who agreed that a new partisan formation with a nucleus of British parachutists could be formed under the Major's command.

Early the next morning, Roy was delighted when, by chance, Victor Pirogov arrived to plead for more arms from Mike Lees. Roy described the Russian as big and blonde, with a charming smile on his face and a captivating swashbuckler's air:

> I put Modena's age at about twenty-seven. He wore a blue, peaked sailor's cap and German jack boots, exactly the costume I would have expected a Russian to wear. Round his neck he had wound a strip of Cambridge blue parachute silk. His horse, which he had captured … was the best in the valley.[1]

Victor inspired devotion amongst his men, most of whom were Mongol deserters from the 162nd Turkoman Infantry Division of the German Army.

From 7–23 March, an Allied Battalion of 300 men was raised, equipped, and trained in the valley. Within three days of his arrival, Roy organised an airdrop of three officers, an instructor and an interpreter to train the Russians and the Italians before the main body of the SAS arrived. The five men landed safely, together with a large quantity of weapons and stores. Roy related: 'This demonstration of power was the prime cause of the success of the operation since it engendered immediate confidence in both Russians and Italians.' On 9 March, a party of twenty-four officers and soldiers arrived. One officer and four soldiers were attached to each of the two local companies.

The battalion consisted of three elements. The British SAS company, which grew to fifty men, was based at the now deserted church at Tapignola. Among the personnel was Company Piper David Kirkpatrick, of the Highland Light Infantry, from Girvan, who dropped on 23 March, wearing his kilt and with the pipes under his arm. He was drafted, Roy recalled, 'to stir the romantic Italian mind and to gratify my own vanity'. Attached to the British were the *Gufo Nero* squad and forty *Garibaldini* under Gianni Farri, ostensibly to receive training in heavy weapons. The Russian company was led by Victor—now using the alias of 'Modena' instead of 'Danilo'. Finally, the battalion absorbed the non-political Military Formation of *Barbanera*. Every man was equipped with battledress, a khaki beret, good boots and a weapon of some description.

Roy Farran was the commandant of the unit, with Annibale Alpi ('*Barbanera*') as deputy and three company commanders—SAS Captain Jock Easton, who was a Scottish escaped prisoner of war, Victor Pirogov ('Modena'), and Remo Torlai ('Tito'). The formation of the battalion was formally approved by the *Comando Unico* on 21 March. Outwardly, the force was under the headquarters' control and expected to receive rations and other assistance, but it was operationally independent.

In view of the difference the addition of British personnel had made to partisan morale in the area, Roy decided to send out detachments with heavy machine guns. The units were under the command of British 'other ranks' and provided three lines of defence in the valley. The battalion carried out numerous operations, but the most significant was an audacious raid on a German headquarters between 25 and 27 March. Mike Lees recalled that the commando-style mission was necessary as an alternative to air strikes that would have damaged the nearby village:

> The Albinea attack was conceived by me at the end of February following a personal reconnaissance of the area and collection of intelligence from the GAP and SAP. I enthusiastically welcomed the offer of SAS help by Roy Farran and subsequently I was absolutely delighted (perhaps even a little relieved) when he made a surprise personal appearance on the stage and offered to take command. On 18 March aerial photographs were dropped to us and around 20 March the British mission received clearance to proceed with the attack.

Led by Roy, a force of twenty-four SAS, twenty of the *Gufo Nero* squad, twenty *Garibaldini* and thirty Russians launched the attack on the headquarters of the 51st German Mountain Corps, housed in two villas at Botteghe in the Commune of Albinea, only 6 miles south of Reggio. Mike Lees insisted on taking part even though he was suffering from a bout of recurrent malaria.

Roy recalled that during the approach march, a courier arrived from Mike's second in command, Lieutenant Smith, who had remained with the radio at Secchio.

> He brought a curt message from Fifteenth Army Group in Florence—our attack was to be postponed for ten days because there had been a change in the plans for the main offensive ... I resolved to pretend the signal failed to reach us in time. Though an attack on the corps headquarters might not have as much effect now as at the time of the main offensive, it would be infinitely better than no attack at all. Lees, who was still running a high fever from malaria, agreed, but the responsibility was mine.[2]

The plan was to infiltrate the men through the enemy positions as soon as it became dark, marching quietly in three tightly-packed columns. They would lie up 10 miles from the target in a farm called Casa del Lupo, and attack at night. The corps' headquarters consisted of two main buildings, and they were separated from the foothills by billets for 300 troops, a prison, a telephone exchange and a guardroom. Villa Calvi housed an operations room and provided accommodation for the Chief of Staff and other senior officers. On the other side of the north–south road was Villa Rossi, the residence of the corps' commander. Ten SAS troops were to force entry to each of the villas, supported by twenty Italians, while the Russians were to form a semi-circular screen to the south to prevent interference by the occupants of the other buildings, spraying the crossroads area indiscriminately with tracer bullets.

The assault on the HQ took place on the night of 26–27 March. The approach march went ahead without incident, despite the start of a German drive in the foothills. The attack columns penetrated the headquarters undetected. Roy directed operations from a slit trench on the roadway between the two main buildings. He recalled:

> My orders were purely for destruction. No prisoners were to be taken because they would only hamper withdrawal. And the main object was to kill German officers and to set fire to their headquarters. The raid was to last no more than twenty minutes and my signal for retreat back to the mountains would be a red Very cartridge fired into the sky.[3]

The firing started first at the Villa Calvi. German troops in the barracks responded with Spandaus. Roy ordered Piper David Kirkpatrick to strike up with 'Highland Laddie' to let the enemy know that they had the British to contend with, but a machine gun picked them out after only a few notes had been played. Roy pushed David into a slit trench and he continued to pipe the men into battle from his cramped position.

The sentries at the Villa Calvi were killed. The front door was locked, but it was soon blown open by a bazooka bomb. Four Germans were killed on the ground floor, but repeated attempts to climb the spiral staircase were rebuffed by concentrated fire from the landing. As it was proving impossible to take the villa in the twenty minutes allotted, a fire was set in the operations room, with explosives and petrol as accelerants. The wounded were carried out to safety while the Germans were kept inside by tommy-gun fire until the whole building was ablaze.

At the Villa Rossi things had not gone so well, as the firing at the other villa was heard before the raiders were in position. A siren gave the alarm from the roof, and all the lights were turned on. The SAS rushed the door and shot out the lights, but a hail of fire greeted them at the foot of the stairs. Two attempts were made to reach the landing, but heavy losses caused them to retreat. The Germans tried to come down, but they withdrew when three of their number were killed. Realising that they were running out of time, the raiders started a fire in the kitchen and evacuated the wounded. Roy pointed his pistol at the sky and fired the red Very light to signal withdrawal.

Thirty Germans were killed in the raid, including the Chief of Staff, Colonel Lemelson. By chance, the commanding artillery general of the 51st Mountain Corps, Friedrich-Wilhelm Hauck, was away on the night. The two main buildings of the headquarters were severely damaged and many maps and papers were destroyed. There were three SAS fatalities—Lieutenant James Arthur Riccomini, MBE, MC, Sergeant Sidney Elliott Guscott, and Corporal Samuel Bolden, MM. Three other Britons were wounded, and six partisans were captured and five wounded. The injured included Captain Lees and 'Gordon'. They were saved by their comrades and eventually evacuated from Parma Province (with the help of local partisans) in the Special Force Fieseler Storch flown by Lieutenant Furio Lauri.

In 1987, Mike Lees told the conference held at Bologna University:

The attack on the German HQ in Albinea in a highly defended zone must rank as one of the most ambitious, organised and daring operations carried out by the Resistance forces. One hundred men were infiltrated more than 30 miles down towards the plains and right inside a HQ directly defended by three hundred troops. What is more, after the action, apart from the three SAS heroes killed in the Villa Rossi, the entire party was got out again, sooner or later, without one single prisoner being taken by the Germans, thanks to the superb leadership of Roy Farran. It was a remarkable feat of arms, of organisation at every level, and above all of cooperation between the SAS under Roy Farran, the British Mission, the partisans from Reggio, the GAP and the SAP.

The concealment and subsequent rescue of Gordon (Glauco Monducci) and myself and the brilliant decision, taken I believe by Gianni Farri, to send us further into the plains towards Reggio—rather than into the foothills which were combed by the Germans—reflected enormous credit on the organisation and courage of the Resistance, of the many Italian civilians involved and of the two SAS troopers who helped carry us away.

Villa Rossi was more than a mere Corps HQ. Effectively it was Army TAC HQ. And Villa Calvi contained the main communications centre and direct telephone and teleprinter link with the *Reich* for all German Forces on that front. I had the good fortune to interview General Hauck in a POW camp near Riccione in 1947 and I know that the attack caused serious disruption to German control and morale apart from giving a very well deserved boost to the confidence of the Resistance.

At 3 a.m. on Easter Sunday, 1 April, and now back in Secchio, Roy was awoken with the news that 200 Germans and Mongols, equipped with mortars, two field guns and horse-drawn transport, had crossed the Secchia at Cavola and penetrated the valley as far as Quara. He rode to the scene and found about twenty partisans from the Catholic Green Flames Brigade on a small knoll 2 miles east of the village. They were exchanging fire with Germans on a similar hillock 200 yards away.

The Major was heartened by the sudden arrival of the new British Liaison Officer, Captain John Lees (no relation to Michael), with twenty of his *Gufo Nero* squad. Roy recalled that the new BLO was similar to his predecessor in many ways—tall, dark, light-hearted, and no man to run at the first whistle of bullets. The two officers conferred and decided that it was likely that the enemy would outflank the outpost at Gatta—held by ten SAS and a Communist brigade—during the night, and therefore endanger the whole partisan force. Only one course of action could save the day.

An urgent message was sent by runner to the Russians at Governara. Victor arrived on horseback at the head of his troops after a three-hour forced march. He took readily to the idea of a counter-attack and deployed his men along the ridge. Roy described the final stage of what became known as the Battle of Ca' Marastoni—Monte della Castagna, and also as the Easter of Blood—as follows:

The ragged line began to move behind me, slowly at first but gathering momentum all the time. The Russians cheered. Their loud hurrahs rang all along the crest and we moved down the slope in a shouting mob towards the enemy. I saw that Stephens and Taylor, who had also made several false starts, were moving them on the right. Our counter-attack was under way.

I may have been wrong—since I was so excited myself and tripped several times over stones, I might well have been—but our numbers seemed to swell. The Italians were particularly inspired by the charge and even outran the Russians, shooting wildly from the hip as they did so. Green Flames appeared from nowhere and, as we gathered momentum, I had the impression that the horde had grown to several hundreds.

It was such a fierce, unstoppable mob of yelling men that it was not surprising when the Germans broke and fled before we reached their positions. Red Very lights, presumably signals of distress or signals to retreat, went up from several points in front of us. I had started in the van but the pace was too much for me and I soon began to lag behind. However, I did see one episode. A group of Germans tried to make a stand in a farmhouse, but the excited partisans ran straight through their bullets, firing from the hip, pumping tracers into the windows. A Green Flame carrying a Bren led a crowd of yelling Russians up to the building. He fired point blank through the window and several Germans came out with their hands up. Two, I remember, were wearing unusual white tunics. The partisans shot them down without mercy. I heard later that two other prisoners were dreadfully mutilated by the Russians, but am unable to say whether the report was true.

It was obvious from the signal flares that the Germans were much more widely dispersed than I had imagined. But it was also clear that they were in full retreat everywhere. I struggled on, trying to keep up with the charge. Our men were now utterly beyond control and I only hoped that the Germans would not attempt to stand on our side of the river. But there was no need to fear. Throwing away their arms, the enemy ran panic-stricken northwards.[4]

The Reggio partisans had defeated a German battalion for the first time. Roy concluded:

By nightfall, not a single enemy soldier remained alive on our side of the Secchia. It was an accomplishment that surprised me no less than the enemy.

After receiving new airdrops of jeeps and taking a 75-mm Howitzer (nicknamed 'Very Tired'), the Allied Battalion transferred to the Modena Valley and carried out numerous attacks on the German supply line along Route 12. They then fought off another German counter-attack near Vallestra and Montefiorino, and, finally, shelled the retreating enemy columns north and west of Sassuolo.

Following the Victory Parade in Modena, the Russian auxiliaries were disarmed and ordered to a holding camp near Reggio, ready for deportation. Roy wrote:

My officers were as horrified as I. But they were glad of one thing of which I only then learned—Modena had already disappeared. None of us were ever to see him again although rumour claimed he opened a small haberdashery shop in Milan.[5]

Whatever the truth of that, by remaining in Italy, Victor avoided the cruel fate meted out to many of the returnees to Stalin's Russia. He was awarded the Italian Silver Medal for Military Valour, and in August 1945 he married one of the female couriers, Nalfa Bonini (known as 'Tatiana'). They had a son, and in 1949 they emigrated to South America—first to Venezuela and then to Argentina, where they also had a daughter.

Roy recalled the aftermath of Operation Tombola:

> Fortunately, I did not receive a trial by court-martial as I expected. The British faction that wanted to try me on two counts—for parachuting behind the lines when forbidden to do so and for attacking the German headquarters at Albinea in contravention of orders—was narrowly defeated, largely through support I received from Colonel Riepe, the US officer at Fifteenth Army Group in charge of special operations. He even went so far as to recommend me for a US Legion of Merit—an ace in the hole because I could hardly be court martialled for something for which I had been decorated. His citation concerning Operation Tombola said that our operations against enemy rear units south of Modena materially assisted the attack of the United States Fourth Corps and contributed significantly to the success of Fifteenth Army Group.
>
> Who dares wins.[6]

Roy Farran became one of the most highly decorated soldiers of the Second World War. As well as the American Legion of Merit, he was awarded the British DSO and the MC with two Bars, and the French *Croix de Guerre*. The partisan leaders at Albinea were also honoured—Giovanni Farri with the American Bronze Star, and Glauco Monducci with the Italian Silver Medal for Military Valour. He was also invited to attend the coronation of Queen Elizabeth II in London in June 1953. Mike Lees was made an honorary citizen of Reggio Emilia in 1949, and of Albinea in 1985, together with the three other leaders. Finally, in 2011, David Kirkpatrick—whose stirring bagpipe music had convinced the Germans that they were under attack by British regular forces, thus avoiding reprisals against the civilian population—was made an honorary citizen of Albinea and of Villa Minozzo.

The guns fell silent in Italy at 2 p.m. on 2 May 1945. The unconditional surrender of all German and Fascist forces had been agreed in secret at

Caserta on 29 April. A constitutional referendum was held on 2 June 1946; as a result, the monarchy was replaced by a republican form of government. On 10 February 1947, the Treaty of Peace with Italy was signed in Paris between Italy and the victorious powers of the Second World War, formally ending hostilities.

Endnotes

Chapter 1

1. Dalton, *The Fateful Years: Memoirs 1931–1945*, (1957), p. 366
2. The memoir by Hugh Dalton, *With British Guns in Italy: A Tribute to Italian Achievement*, was published by Methuen of London in 1919

Chapter 2

1. The National Archives (TNA): WO 224/178, *Italy, Location of Camps and Strengths*
2. TNA: AIR 40/1897, *The Return of Escapers and Evaders up to 30 June 1945 by areas, services and nationalities*
3. Churchill, *The Second World War Volume V: Closing the Ring* (1985), pp. 166–167
4. Franzini, *Gli stranieri nella Resistenza in Emilia-Romagna*, (1977)
5. Battaglia, *The Story of the Italian Resistance*, (1957), pp. 9–10

Chapter 3

1. Churchill, *op. cit.*, p. 440
2. Lamb, *War in Italy 1943–1945: A Brutal Story*, (1995), p. 228

Chapter 4

1. Letter from Dott. Enzo Savorgnan, Prefect for Reggio Emilia, to the Ministry of the Interior, *Aggression on soldiers of the service by an armed band*, (27 October 1943)

Chapter 5

1. Letter from Captain Domenico Carbone, Commandant of the Reggio Emilia *Carabinieri* Company, to the Ministry of the Interior and many superior commands, *Disarmament of some of the personnel at the station of S. Martino in Rio*, (7 November 1943)
2. Cervi and Nicolai, *I miei sette figli*, (2001), p. 113
3. Veroni, 'Considerazioni sui Cervi', in *Ricerche Storiche*, No. 38/39, (December 1979)
4. Cervi and Nicolai, *op. cit.*, p. 136

Chapter 6

1. Mander, *Mander's March on Rome*, (1987), p. 22
2. Escape Report in TNA: WO 208/3321
3. Mander, *op. cit.*, p. 107
4. *Ibid.*, p. 115
5. *Ibid.*, p. 144
6. *Ibid.*, p. 146

Chapter 7

1. Hood, *Pebbles from my Skull*, (1973), p. 26
2. *Ibid.*, p. 39
3. *Ibid.*, p. 49
4. *Ibid.*, p. 54
5. *Ibid.*, p. 120

Chapter 8

1. Correspondence with the author
2. *Ibid.*
3. Corvo, *The OSS in Italy 1942–1945: A Personal Memoir*, (1990), p. 203
4. Windsor, *The Mouth of the Wolf*, (1967), pp. 141–142
5. *Ibid.*, pp. 159–160
6. *Ibid.*, p. 167
7. *Ibid.*, p. 170

Chapter 9

1. Pickering and Hart, *The Bandits of Cisterna*, (1991), pp. 2–3

Chapter 10

1. Tompkins, 'The OSS and Italian Partisans in World War II', in *Studies in Intelligence*, (Spring 1998)

Chapter 11

1. Correspondence with the author
2. Lett, *Rossano*, (1956), p. 124

Chapter 12

1. References are to the BLO's report on Liguria by Lieutenant Colonel R. P. McMullen, DSO, MBE, in TNA: HS 6/843
2. Hastings, *The Drums of Memory: An Autobiography*, (2001), p. 115
3. Davidson, *Special Operations Europe: Scenes from the Anti-Nazi War*, (1987), pp. 279–280
4. *Ibid.*, p. 292
5. *Ibid.*, p. 333
6. *Ibid.*, p. 339
7. *Ibid.*, pp. 363–364

Chapter 13

1. Warren, *Special Operations: AAF Aid to European Resistance Movements 1943–1945*, (1947)

Chapter 14

1. TNA: Document MI9/WEA/2572/1654
2. Correspondence with the author
3. *Ibid.*

Chapter 15

1. McMullen, *op. cit.*
2. Hastings, *op. cit.*, p. 129

Chapter 16

1. Farran, *Winged Dagger: Adventures on Special Service*, (1998), p. 282
2. Farran, *Operation Tombola*, (1986), pp. 95–96
3. *Ibid.*, p. 85
4. *Ibid.*, pp. 138–139
5. *Ibid.*, p. 254
6. *Ibid.*, pp. 255–256

Bibliography

Battaglia, R., *The Story of the Italian Resistance* (London: Odhams, 1957)

Cervi, A., and Nicolai, R., *I miei sette figli* (Rome: Editore Riuniti, 2001)

Churchill, W. S., *The Second World War Volume V: Closing the Ring* (London: Book Club Associates, 1985)

Corvo, M., *The OSS in Italy 1942–1945: A Personal Memoir* (New York: Praeger, 1990)

Dalton, H., *The Fateful Years: Memoirs 1931–1945* (London: Frederick Muller, 1957)

Davidson, B., *Special Operations Europe: Scenes from the Anti-Nazi War* (London: Grafton Books, 1987)

Farran, R., *Operation Tombola* (London: Arms and Armour Press, 1986); *Winged Dagger, Adventures on Special Service* (London: Cassell, 1998)

Franzini, G., *Gli stranieri nella resistenza in Emilia-Romagna* (Reggio Emilia: Comitato Provinciale ANPI e l'Istituto storico della Resistenza, 1977)

Hastings, S., *The Drums of Memory: An Autobiography* (Barnsley: Leo Cooper, 2001)

Hood, S., *Pebbles from my Skull* (London: Quartet Books, 1973)—new edition published as *Carlino* (Manchester: Carcanet Press, 1985)

Istituto per la storia della Resistenza e della Guerra di Liberazione, Ricerche Storiche, No. 38/39 (Reggio Emilia: December 1979)

Lamb, R., *War in Italy 1943–1945: A Brutal Story* (London: Penguin Books, 1995)

Lett, G., *Rossano* (London: Hamilton and Co., 1956)

Mander, D., *Mander's March on Rome* (Gloucester: Alan Sutton Publishing, 1987)

Pickering, W., with Hart, A., *The Bandits of Cisterna* (London: Leo Cooper, 1991)

'Records of the Central Intelligence Agency', *Studies in Intelligence* (Spring 1998)

Tarasov, A., *Sui monti d'italia: Memorie di un garibaldino russo* (Leningrad: Lenizdat, 1960)

Warren, H. G., *Special Operations: AAF Aid to European Resistance Movements 1943–1945* (US Air Force Historical Study No. 121, 1947)

Windsor, J., *The Mouth of the Wolf* (London: Hodder and Stoughton, 1967)